House Plants

By the Garden Editors
of Southern Living Magazine

Library of Congress Catalog Card Number: 75-12123
ISBN: 0-8487-0384-7

Manufactured in the United States of America
Fifth Printing 1982

House Plants

Cover Photograph: Taylor Lewis
Illustrations: Ralph Mark
Photography: Jack Goodson, Bob Lancaster, Joe Benton, &
    Bert O'Neal

Advisory panel:

Fred C. Galle
Director of Horticulture
Callaway Gardens
Pine Mountain, Georgia

Floyd A. Giles
Extension Horticulturist
Illinois Cooperative Extension Service
Urbana, Illinois

Kenneth R. Scott
Extension Horticulturist
Arkansas Cooperative Extension Service
Little Rock, Arkansas

Ronald L. Shumack
Ornamental Horticulturist
Alabama Cooperative Extension Service
Auburn, Alabama

Contents

List of Plant Photographs

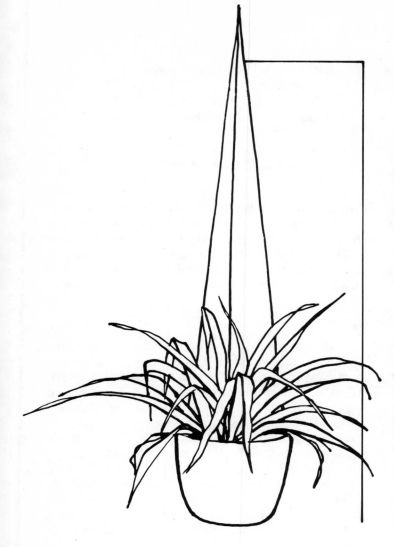

Introduction

Welcome to the world of house plants. It is a different world from that of outdoor gardening. The indoor environment is easier to control and manipulate, allowing us to bring tropical and desert plants into the same room, even in places where the outdoor climate may support only Arctic mosses and lichens.

This is not to say that plants have no difficulty surviving indoors. The air in our homes is drier than most plants like, especially during the winter when we must rely on artificial heating. But simple devices such as plastic sandwich bags can help a struggling plant adjust to the indoors.

Decorating with house plants is easier and less expensive than decorating with paintings or antique furniture. There is no faster way of altering the character of a room or of an entire house than by adding plants. A bare wall can become the home of a staghorn fern, or a free-standing plant rack can make an interesting room partition. Porches and decks can become lush and verdant with the addition of hanging baskets.

Keeping plants, like keeping children or pets, entails certain responsibilities. *House Plants* provides the amateur plantsman with the information he or she will need to keep plants alive and thriving. In addition, we have included tips on how to display plants effectively in the home, how to make hanging baskets and terrariums, and how to handle special plants such as ferns, cactus, and bromeliads. Wherever possible, cultural information is presented in chart form so that the reader may see at a glance the water, light, fertilizing, repotting, temperature, and humidity needs of a particular plant.

Plants have Latin names as well as English names. Because the English name may vary significantly from one area to another, we include also the Latin name in order to assure precise identification of plants you may wish to acquire. In the case of many plants, such as dracaena, English and Latin names are the same. But to distinguish the dracaena with spike-like leaves from the one with wide leaves that droop by using the names *Dracaena marginata* and *Dracaena fragrans* will enable the retailer to better assist you. To provide the most widely known English plant names, we have chosen *Standardized Plant Names* as our authority. Where this was not possible we have referred to *Wyman's Gardening Encyclopedia* and *Hortus Third*.

Getting Started

You're already started; you obviously have some interest in house plants. The next thing you need is a plant.

We are fortunate to live in an age when even the most exotic tropical plants are available to anyone who wants them. Most common house plants are, in fact, tropical plants that will accept the untropical conditions of our homes. Desert plants, such as cactus and echeveria, have become popular house plants as have a number of ferns. These facts lead logically to the question, what is a house plant? The answer is, any plant that can be grown indoors. Broad as this answer may seem, the fact is that not all plants can be grown under the dry, shaded conditions found in the home. As your gardening knowledge and skills increase, however, so will your ability to grow more difficult plants indoors with success.

There are a number of ways to obtain house plants. You may receive one as a gift, someone may give you a cutting from a plant, or you can simply buy a plant.

Easy plants for beginners

Though the following list is not exhaustive, the plants recommended here are considered easy to grow and will thrive under difficult growing conditions:

Aspidistra, Cast-iron plant
Chinese evergreen
Dieffenbachia, Dumb cane
Dracaena, Corn plant
English ivy
Maranta, Prayer plant
Nephthytis, African evergreen
Peperomia
Philodendron (*P. cordatum*)
Piggyback plant, Pick-a-back plant
Rubber plant
Sansevieria, Snake plant
Spathiphyllum (Peace plant)

In addition to the above, a number of plants known as *succulents* (mostly desert plants with thick, fleshy, succulent leaves) are considered easy to grow. Some plants in this category include echeveria, jade plant, euphorbia, sedum, cotyledon, and cactus. These plants are well suited to the home environment because they tolerate hot, dry conditions.

Buying plants

The best place to buy plants from is a reputable greenhouse or nursery. Though the plants may be more expensive, your chances of getting a quality plant are better. Supermarkets and other stores frequently offer house plants, especially around holidays, but a supermarket cannot provide the greenhouse conditions that are conducive to optimum plant growth. Another distinct advantage in dealing with a greenhouse is that you are also buying the advice of a professional plantsman who can tell you where to locate your plants and how to care for them. If you do buy supermarket plants, try to get them as soon after they are unpacked as possible.

Purchase only healthy plants. If the plant is already damaged or blemished when you bring it home, chances are it will get worse before it gets better. Be certain you can provide the conditions required by the plants you select. Don't be afraid to ask the nurseryman about the plant's lighting, watering, and fertilizing needs.

Transporting plants home

It is always a good idea to wrap plants in newspaper or to place them in paper bags to transport them home. During very cold weather, wrap the plants first in plastic, then in several thicknesses of paper. Plants must be protected against extreme temperatures and wind. During the summer, a paper covering will protect the plant against sunscald. During clement spring or fall weather, plants will not require such precautions.

Once home, do not immediately place new plants with other plants in your home. Keep them segregated for at least 4 or 5 days and inspect them daily until you are satisfied that they carry no insects or diseases that could spread to other plants. Inspect undersides of leaves as well as upper surfaces. When you are certain the plants are pest free and healthy, locate them where their light, temperature, and humidity requirements will be met (see Chapter Two, *Caring For House Plants*).

If you should discover insect or disease problems on your new plants, return them immediately to the place of purchase. You will be doing the retailer a favor by letting him know about an insect or disease infestation he may not have detected.

Other sources of plants

Gift plants. Plants are popular gifts. Many people receive poinsettias, Christmas cactus, or kalanchoe for Christmas, azaleas for Valentine's Day, and lilies for Easter. For the plant enthusiast, a plant makes a splendid gift at any time of the year.

If you are a beginner and you have just received a gift plant, don't discard it as soon as it finishes blooming; it may well be that you can enjoy the plant again—and have the satisfaction of reblooming it yourself.

Cuttings. Many house plants will grow from cuttings or "slips." Place cuttings in sharp sand or perlite until they form roots. Some house plants will root in a jar of water. After roots have formed, put the plants in a suitable potting soil (see Chapter Five, *Propagating House Plants*). Never take cuttings from public or botanical gardens. The plants are there for all to enjoy, and a poorly made cutting can damage the plant. But don't hesitate to ask friends for cuttings. Wrap a damp tissue around the cut stem and put it in a plastic bag, if possible, to keep it moist until you get it home. Depending on the plant, take leaf cuttings, stem cuttings, or sections from the main stem. For a list of plants suited to this method of propagation, see Chapter Five, *Propagating House Plants*. Once the cuttings have formed roots, pot them in packaged soil from the garden supply store or make your own potting medium by mixing equal parts garden loam, peat moss, and sand or perlite. This soil suits most plants.

Potted outdoor plants. Many outdoor plants can be removed from the ground in the fall, potted, and brought indoors for the winter. Dig individual plants or clumps of plants carefully, trying to keep some soil attached to the roots. This additional soil will help the plant become established in its container. Select a container that will accommodate the root ball rather than stuff the roots into a small container. Relocate potted plants gradually, leaving them out-

doors for 2 or 3 days before bringing them in. Keep the soil slightly moist.

The following plants can be potted for sunny locations indoors:

> Aster
> Bromeliad
> Cactus (if you live in the Southwest)
> Chrysanthemum
> Coleus
> Daisy
> Daylily
> Geranium
> Impatiens
> Iris
> Marigold
> Periwinkle
> Spanish moss (requires no soil)
> Yucca (small ones)
> Zinnia (use sterilized soil)

Plants from the kitchen. Seed for a number of plants suited for indoor culture can be found in the grocery bag. Sweet potatoes, avocados, and pineapple tops can form roots and grow into interesting house plants. Grapefruit, lemon, orange, and other citrus plants are easy to grow from seed found in the fresh fruit. Peaches, plums, and cherries all carry viable seed, but the seeds must be dried, wrapped in damp peat moss, and stored in the refrigerator for 2 to 6 months before they can germinate (sprout). Fruit trees can be very rewarding house plants, but their culture is exacting and not always successful.

Cut off the top of the pineapple, making an even slice. Place the top in a jar of water. After roots have formed, pot the plant in regular potting soil.

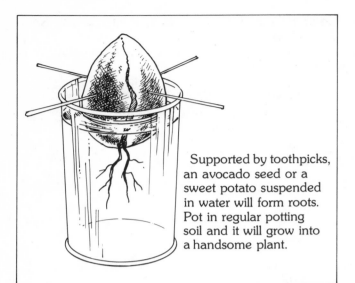

Supported by toothpicks, an avocado seed or a sweet potato suspended in water will form roots. Pot in regular potting soil and it will grow into a handsome plant.

Garden plants in pots. A great number of outdoor garden plants can be grown from seed planted in pots (see Chapter Five, *Propagating House Plants*). Many florist plants, such as chrysanthemum and impatiens, can be easily grown indoors in containers if you can provide a sunny location. Annuals such as marigold, zinnia, and sweet alyssum adapt easily to indoor culture. Lantana, chrysanthemum, and geranium are among those garden perennials that grow well indoors. Bulbous plants for the indoor gardener include crocus, daffodil, hyacinth, and tulip (see Chapter Nine, *Bulbs*).

Zinnia 'Hot Buttons', a good annual to grow in a container.

Mail-order plants. You will find a great many house plants advertised by mail-order houses in home and garden magazines. Prices are often good and special insect and disease precautions are required of firms that ship plants from one state to another.

Spring and fall are the best times to buy mail-order plants. The extreme temperatures of winter and summer are unfavorable to the shipment of house plants.

Be prepared to pot mail-order plants as soon as you receive them. This will help the plants recover quickly from travel and lack of light. Do not expose plants to direct sunlight at the outset; allow them to adjust gradually to their new surroundings. (For potting instructions, see Chapter Two, *Caring For House Plants.*)

Once they are potted, keep new plants segregated from other plants for a few days to be certain they are free from pests and diseases.

A sweet potato vine is a striking plant for a hanging basket.

Caring for House Plants

Locating plants in the correct light

Some plants need more light than others. Many tropical plants, whose native habitat is the jungle, are accustomed to growing in the dense shade cast by giant trees. Other plants, such as cacti, are accustomed to the scorching sun. For purposes of discussion, we may describe four types of light situations found in homes: direct sun, full light, medium light, and low light.

Direct sun. Plants requiring direct sun should be placed in a south-facing window where they will receive sunlight for at least 4 hours a day. Many flowering plants, such as chrysanthemums or geraniums, require direct sunlight.

Full light. Many plants need a bright, airy environment but will get scorched if placed in direct sunlight. A room with southern exposure is usually bright enough, unless buildings are so close together that considerable light is screened. Direct sunlight filtered through a curtain also provides the right amount of light for plants that require full light.

Medium light. Most rooms in the home have medium light. The more shaded areas of a well-lighted room may also have medium light. Many plants that require full light for optimum growth will adapt to medium light to sustain healthy but slower growth.

Low light. Rooms such as bathrooms and bedrooms usually receive less light than kitchens and living areas. Although the difference in lighting may not seem significant to us, many plants would have difficulty surviving in the more subdued light. Happily, a surprising number of plants grow in low light; among them are cast-iron plant, Chinese evergreen, dieffenbachia, dracaena, philodendron, sansevieria, peace plant, and brake fern.

Natural light can be supplemented by the use of artificial light.

Using fluorescent lighting

Most house plants can be grown successfully under ordinary fluorescent lamps. Especially designed full-spectrum fluorescent lamps are also available. In homes where exposure to natural sunlight is inadequate for house plants, artificial lighting may solve the problem. Plants grown under fluorescent lamps receive a uniform amount of light over a longer period of the day (12 to 16 hours). Because the soil does not dry out as quickly under artificial light, plants require less frequent watering. The risk of scorching foliage is eliminated; most plants can be placed within 6 inches of fluorescent lamps without being damaged.

Fluorescent lamp fixtures may be mounted on a table or plant stand where plants are located, or you may prefer to build a planter with lamps mounted on it. One advantage of a planter is that pots can be concealed to give the planter a more natural look. Equip the planter with casters so that it can be moved to facilitate cleaning under and around it.

Whatever the type of planter you select, you can easily obtain lamps and mounting fixtures at electrical supply houses. Fixtures with white or silver backs will redirect and increase the light in the growing area. Place lamps so that light is directed toward the plants but not toward the room in which the planter

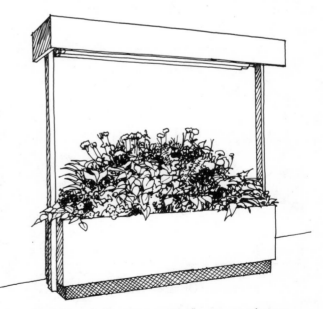

A planter such as this, with fluorescent lamps mounted at the top, can be the answer for rooms that receive too little light for healthy plant growth.

is located. The glare emitted by fluorescent lamps can be bothersome to some people.

Attach a 24-hour timer to the lamps rather than trying to remember to turn them off and on at the proper times. With a timer, you can be assured that plants are receiving the correct amount of light, even when you are away from home for a few days. During vacations and other times when you will be away for more than just a day or two, reduce lighting to about 10 hours a day. A slight reduction in light will also reduce water and fertilizer needs.

Two standard 40-watt fluorescent lamps provide enough light for most foliage house plants. Flowering plants may require more. Citrus, gardenia, geranium, gloxinia, and others will flower properly only with the use of high-output fluorescent lamps. Place plants whose light requirements are high within 6 to 12 inches of the lamps.

To measure light in a given location as precisely as possible, you may want to purchase a light meter at the garden supply store.

The standard measure of light is the *footcandle*. A footcandle is the amount of light cast by one candle on a surface of 1 foot away. The following graph will give a good idea of the amount of light shed at distances from 6 to 36 inches by two 40-watt lamps. The second graph measures the amount of light shed by two 150-watt fluorescent lamps.

Keep the surfaces of the lamps clean to assure maximum efficiency of the lighting system. After 18 to 24 months, depending on the amount of use, the lamps will need to be replaced. Replace them one at a time to allow a brief period of adjustment (100 to 150 hours) which fluorescent lamps require to reach peak efficiency. New lamps may perform erratically and to replace them both at the same time could result in damage to the plants.

Temperature and humidity

Plants often suffer from the high temperatures in most homes. More adverse than the temperature, however, is the dryness of the air indoors, especially during the winter. Moisture in house plant soil evaporates quickly both night and day whereas moisture in the form of dew would tend to settle at night on outdoor plants. Compensation can be made for both the temperature and humidity conditions in our homes.

First, do not locate plants above radiators, registers, or other outlets for artificial heating. The direct flow of hot, dry air on the plants will cause their rapid demise.

Windows are ideal locations for many plants because they are cooler at night than other locations in the same room. A night temperature of 60° is good for most house plants. Before locating plants in windows, however, be certain that the light conditions during the day are correct for the plant you wish to locate there.

Humidity can be increased anywhere in a room

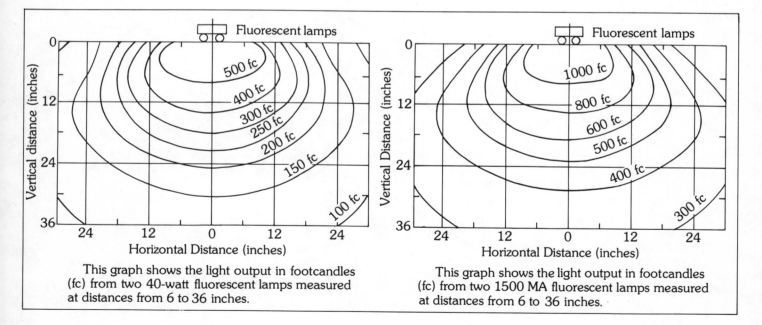

This graph shows the light output in footcandles (fc) from two 40-watt fluorescent lamps measured at distances from 6 to 36 inches.

This graph shows the light output in footcandles (fc) from two 1500 MA fluorescent lamps measured at distances from 6 to 36 inches.

by placing plants on a tray of gravel and water. Fill a shallow tray with 1-inch gravel or pebbles and fill the tray with water so that plant containers may be set on the pebbles without being in contact with the water. Otherwise water will be drawn up through the drainage hole in the bottom of the container and will keep the soil too wet.

Locating plants above sinks provides a humid environment for the plants and an added interest to kitchens and bathrooms.

To raise humidity around a plant, fill a tray with pebbles. Next, pour water into the tray until it is nearly even with the top of the pebbles. Place potted plants on the tray; the water evaporating from the tray will moisten the air around the foliage.

Watering house plants

The greatest cause of house plant mortality is improper watering. Overwatering is more fatal than underwatering, but both can do considerable damage to plants. Symptoms for both extremes are similar—wilting and decline. Most plants can recover easily from minor wilting due to lack of water, but plants whose roots are left standing in water for prolonged periods cannot conduct oxygen through those roots to the rest of the plant. The suffocating

effect on the plant is much like drowning for mammals.

The first rule, then, in watering house plants is to apply water only when it is needed. Learn to gauge the moisture content of the soil by its color and feel. The drier the soil becomes, the lighter it is in color. If moisture is not added, the soil surface becomes cracked and tends to pull away from the sides of the container. At this stage or sooner, wilting occurs. Water plants before they wilt. When the surface of the soil crumbles between your fingers, apply water.

Some plants require more water than others. Spathiphyllum and most ferns, for example, need water every 2 to 4 days. Flowering plants generally require more water than foliage plants, especially during the growing season; but even with these, water only when the soil or the plants indicate a need for moisture.

A number of factors can affect the moisture needs of plants. Evaporation is more rapid in a warm, dry room than in a cool room. The type of potting soil makes a difference; some potting media are moisture retentive due to the addition of peat or sphagnum moss whereas sandy potting soils allow water to drain through faster. The container used also influences the frequency of watering. Clay containers absorb a great deal of moisture and permit rapid evaporation; plastic, ceramic, or metal containers retain moisture without absorbing it. Water plants in plastic containers only half as frequently as those in clay containers.

Double potting. Overwatering is less likely to occur if plants are double potted. This method provides moisture to the plant through the sides of the pot. Only porous pots, such as those made from clay or peat, should be double potted.

After potting the plant in a clay or other porous pot, set the pot inside a large, watertight container and fill the space between the containers with sphagnum moss. Raise the height of the clay pot, if necessary, by putting coarse gravel in the bottom of the outside container. Water the soil inside the clay pot and the moss outside it. As the plant needs moisture, it can draw water through the walls of the clay pot. Double potting also retards loss of moisture through evaporation through the sides of an exposed pot.

Double potting is especially helpful with plants requiring a low level of soil moisture or with plants growing in dim light. Because the soil dries slowly, frequency of watering is not as critical as it is when plants are grown in pots exposed to air.

Plastic, metal, or ceramic containers cannot be

11

Double potting makes watering easier. Fill the bottom of a large pot with pebbles or broken pottery. Place the pot containing the plant inside the larger pot and fill in around it with sphagnum moss. Keep the moss moist. Water applied to the moss will seep through the sides of clay pots and keep the soil around the roots evenly moist.

double potted because these materials do not allow the passage of moisture and air.

Do not apply excessively warm or cold water to plants. Water should be room temperature or lukewarm. Tap water is fine for house plants in most sections of the United States. In cities where the water contains a great deal of chlorine, the water should be left to sit overnight in an uncovered container before being applied to the plants. This allows some of the chlorine to evaporate. Water from water softeners should not be used at all.

The best water for plants, both indoors and out, is rainwater. Rainwater contains plant nutrients and is free from chlorination and other purification treatment. It is not difficult to collect rainwater; any large container that can be left outdoors or on the patio or deck is sufficient. If your home has rain gutters and downspouts, collecting water will be be simple.

The most common method of watering is from the top of the pot. The water then seeps into the root zone. When watering by this method, keep the flow of water gentle to avoid washing soil away from roots and to avoid splashing water onto the leaves. Water splashed onto foliage often encourages the spread of diseases. A watering can is the best device for watering indoor plants. The long spout of the

can allows you to water gently and to direct the flow of water exactly where you want it.

Avoid wetting the crown (junction of roots and stems) of plants as this may encourage crown rot. Direct the flow of water around the walls of the container. Water will then seep toward the center of the pot under the surface.

However, watering from the top of the pot is not the only method of irrigating house plants. Sometimes subirrigating is better, especially for young plants.

Subirrigating, or watering a plant from the bottom up, allows potting soil to absorb water without being compacted or washed around. The potting soil acts as a sponge, drawing moisture into the entire root ball. Set the pot in a container of water for 15 to 20 minutes while water is drawn up through the drainage hole in the bottom of the pot. Pots or other containers without adequate drainage holes must be watered from the top. When the soil in the pot appears saturated, remove the pot from the water and allow excess water to drain. This method permits an even distribution of moisture throughout the root zone and at the same time avoids splashing water on foliage. However, subirrigating permits the build-up of salts on the soil surface. When this occurs, scrape the white crust from the surface and water from the top to wash the salts out of the soil.

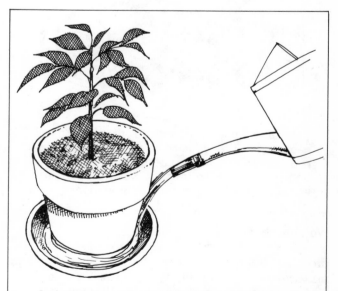

Soil absorbs water like a sponge. Water applied to a saucer under the pot is drawn up through the drainage hole in the bottom of the pot. This method of watering is called *subirrigating* or watering from the bottom.

Misting or *foliar watering* means spraying the foliage with a fine mist of water. This is recommended for humidity-loving plants such as ferns, citrus, and many others. Plants in a warm, dry location may require light misting daily. Do not mist cacti or plants with pubescent (hairy) leaves such as African violet. A simple spray bottle makes an excellent misting device.

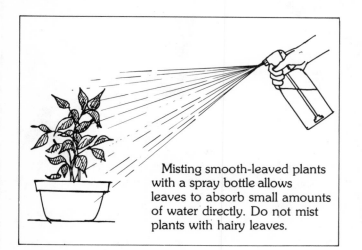

Misting smooth-leaved plants with a spray bottle allows leaves to absorb small amounts of water directly. Do not mist plants with hairy leaves.

Most house plants fall roughly into three watering categories: plants which require frequent watering, plants which require medium watering, and plants which require light watering. The first group should be kept fairly moist (but not soaked) all the time. Plants that require medium watering should be watered about once a week. Water the plants slowly until water drains from the bottom of the container, then allow the soil to become moderately dry before watering again. Most house plants are watered in this manner. Light moisture plants, such as cacti and succulents, should receive nearly as much water per application as medium moisture plants, but apply the water less frequently. For cacti too much water is a certain death.

During the winter, water plants less frequently. This is a period of rest for most plants during which they are particularly susceptible to damage resulting from overwatering. Cacti and other succulents should be watered only enough to keep them from shriveling.

However, high room temperatures do encourage the loss of moisture through evaporation. Each winter, many house plants die in the hot, arid living rooms of artificially heated homes. Thus, double potting is especially recommended for plants whose moisture and humidity requirements are high.

Repotting house plants

House plants must be repotted when their roots become restricted and matted on the outside of the root ball. Some plants require repotting more frequently than others. In general, fast-growing plants may need to be repotted twice a year. Most plants require repotting only once a year and some won't need repotting for two or three years.

A number of flowering plants, such as African violet, geranium, and begonia, grow best when they are slightly pot-bound (have crowded roots), but these are the exception.

The best time to repot overcrowded plants is in the spring as new growth begins. However, many plants can be safely repotted at any time of the year. Do not wait until spring to repot severely crowded plants; they may die from root strangulation before spring arrives.

Check plants whose roots you suspect may be crowded. If plants wilt quickly between waterings and growth is generally slow and stunted, repotting may be necessary. If roots begin to protrude through the drainage hole in the bottom of the pot or appear on the surface of the soil, the plant needs to be repotted. The surest method of finding out is to remove the plant from the pot to inspect the root ball. Moisten the soil slightly to make it cohere, then tip the pot upside down to slide the plant out. If it does not come readily, tap the side of the pot gently. If the roots are matted around the outside of the soil ball, the plant must be repotted.

After removing the plant from its pot, carefully loosen the larger roots that are matted, but do not crumble the soil ball. Remove any roots that have rotted.

Repotting does not necessarily mean going to a larger container. Mature plants that might become difficult to handle if allowed to grow any larger should have their roots pruned and be repotted in the same size container. Cut back the top growth to maintain a balance between roots and top. If roots are cut but the amount of top growth the roots must support is not, the roots will have greater difficulty recovering from the shock of being pruned. For young plants, however, select a container at least 2 inches larger in diameter, then cover the drainage hole with a small piece of crockery from a broken pot. Fill the bottom of the pot with 1 inch of pebbles or gravel to assure good drainage.

Add enough potting soil so that the top of the root ball, when placed in the pot, will be about 1 inch below the rim of the pot. Fill in around the sides of the root ball with potting soil, and firm it with a

Repotting Plants

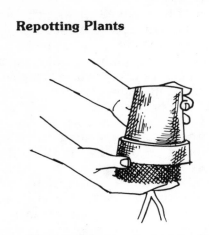

Moisten soil, then turn pot upside down to remove the plant. If it does not slide right out, gently tap the side of the pot. Trim excess growth off roots severely matted around the root ball.

Fill the bottom of the new pot with pebbles or 1-inch gravel. Add 1 inch of potting soil and set the plant in the pot. Adjust soil underneath until the top of the root ball is 1 inch lower than the rim of the pot. Fill in around the root ball with soil, tamping it gently in place with a small stick. Water the plant to settle the soil.

A side view of the potted plant. If repotting is done because the plant is root-bound, select a new pot at least 2 inches larger in diameter than the old one.

tamping stick. Water the new soil gently to settle it, then add more soil as needed to bring the level of the soil up to the top of the root ball. Do not fill the pot to the rim; water and soil will be washed over the sides when you are watering the plants.

Large plants are often troublesome to repot. Trees, shrubs, and other plants large enough to require tubs can be kept in the same container for several years if they are top-dressed. Top-dressing consists of removing the upper 2 inches of soil, including roots, and replacing it with fresh potting soil.

Potting new plants

Plants purchased from mail-order houses or cuttings you have rooted must be potted. Select a container with good drainage. Different plants may require different potting soils, but most grow well in a mixture of equal parts peat moss, garden loam, and sand or perlite (see *Soil For House Plants*).

Do not cramp the roots together. They should be spread out as much as possible to encourage their rapid establishment. If the roots reach the walls of the container, the container is too small. Potting plants in too small a container hampers their development. They will also need to be repotted sooner. Fill the container with soil to 1 inch below the rim, firm it, and water thoroughly.

Soil for house plants

Most common house plants grow well in a *loamy soil mix,* consisting of equal parts garden loam, peat moss, and sand or perlite. Mix the soil outside or on newspaper to minimize the clean up chores. Sift the mixed soil through ¼-inch screen to remove rocks, sticks, and clods.

Cacti and succulents prefer a *light, sandy soil* that is well drained. These desert plants cannot stand excessive moisture around their roots. Mix 2 parts sand with 1 part loam and 1 part peat moss for most cacti and succulents.

Ferns and tropical plants which require a great deal of moisture grow best in peaty soil. Mix 2 parts peat moss or leaf mold with 1 part loam and 1 part sand or perlite. Some plants in this class will grow extremely well in sphagnum moss alone.

Soil for house plants should be sterilized to kill any disease organisms or weed seeds that may be present in the soil. Fill a shallow pan with soil mix and bury a potato in the center. Bake in the oven at 180°. When the potato is cooked, the soil will be sterile. You can mix soil yourself or buy sterilized potting soil at the garden supply store.

Pots should also be sterilized. Clay, metal, or ceramic containers can be baked in the oven along with pans of soil being sterilized. Plastic or cane basket containers that would melt or burn in the oven can be sterilized by dipping them in a solution of 1 part liquid household bleach to 9 parts water. Let them dry before putting soil in them.

Plants to grow in sphagnum moss. Some plants grow well in sphagnum moss alone (available at garden supply stores), and therefore do not require that you make the effort to mix soils. Like packaged potting soils, packaged sphagnum moss is sterile. Such a peaty medium is very moisture retentive and plants grown in it require less frequent watering. The following plants grow well in sphagnum moss:

Azalea
Chinese evergreen
Dieffenbachia
Gardenia
Monstera
Philodendron
Wax plant

Plants to grow in water. A few plants will grow in water alone. Change water every week to prevent plants and water from becoming rancid. Add ¼ teaspoon of mild liquid fertilizer per quart of fresh water every other time you change it. The following plants grow well in a container with 1 to 2 inches of water:

Chinese evergreen
Coleus
Cordyline, Hawaiian ti plant
English ivy
Philodendron *(P. cordatum)*
Scindapsus, Devil's ivy
Swedish ivy
Wandering Jew

Fertilizing house plants

Fertilizer supplies nutrients that are essential to plant growth. Plants must have nitrogen, phosphorus, and potassium, as well as a number of other elements to sustain life.

There are essentially two approaches to feeding house plants: frequent, light fertilization or occasional fertilization (once every 3 or 4 months) in a somewhat heavier dosage. Frequent, light fertilization results in vigorous growth whereas feeding at greater intervals results in slower growing plants that require less water, less light, and less frequent grooming and repotting. Fast growing plants generally require more attention than those whose rate of

growth is slower. There is, of course, something to be said for either method, depending on just how much time you have to spend with your plants.

Newly purchased plants have very likely been fertilized recently and should need no fertilizer for six months. Be careful not to over-fertilize house plants. The tiny hair roots of plants may be severely damaged by concentrations of fertilizer in the soil. Furthermore, the rapid growth sometimes stimulated by overfertilizing is spindly and weak.

Do not fertilize plants during the winter months; this is a period of rest in the annual cycle of many plants. Exceptions to this rule include plants that bloom in the winter or that bloom year round.

Liquid fertilizer, available at garden supply centers, is the easiest to use and to store. You can also make liquid fertilizer solution at home by adding 1½ teaspoons of concentrated, water soluble fertilizer, such as 20-20-20, to 1 gallon of water. Fertilizer for liquid solutions must be soluble in water, that is, able to dissolve in water. Apply the solution at the rate of ¼ cup to a 6-inch plant pot; apply ½ cup to an 8-inch pot; and 1 cup to a 10-inch pot. Fish emulsion is also a recommended fertilizer and is available commercially.

As with all garden chemicals, keep fertilizer out of the reach of children and pets.

Apply mild solutions of fertilizer once every 2 to 4 weeks. The more frequent the feeding, the weaker the dosage should be.

To promote slower growth, especially for large plants, fertilize once every 3 to 6 months, depending on the plant. Slow-release fertilizers are available at the garden supply center. The best approach to fertilizing plants on a low maintenance schedule is to feed them only when they show signs of a need for fertilizer.

Common symptoms of nutrient deficiency in plants include yellowing of leaves, a general dullness of color, and perhaps even the loss of some leaves. However, if plants exhibit these symptoms, be sure that under-fertilization is the problem before adding more fertilizer. Overwatered plants or plants whose roots have become pot-bound may also exhibit these signs. Check the root ball for moistness and for excessive root growth around the outside of the soil ball. When you do add fertilizer, do so with care, applying it in small doses until you are satisfied that the plant did need feeding. Applying unneeded fertilizer to a plant whose health is less than good will almost surely worsen the situation.

If fertilizer begins to accumulate and to form a crust on the surface of the soil, gently scrape it off and replace whatever soil you have removed with fresh potting soil. Water thoroughly from the top of the pot to wash salts and excess fertilizer out of the soil. Plants that are watered by immersion or by subirrigation are especially prone to such surface accumulations.

Grooming house plants

A few routine practices will keep your house plants looking their best. The leaves of most foliage plants should be wiped with a wet sponge or cloth from time to time to remove accumulations of dust and to maintain the glossy appearance of such plants as schefflera, rubber plant, dracaena, dieffenbachia, and other broadleaf, smooth foliage plants. Do not wash plants with pubescent (hairy) foliage, and do not remove the powdery coating on succulents such as echeveria. Plants with pubescent foliage should be brushed occasionally, however, to remove dust and other grime that may accumulate. Use a soft brush, such as a baby's hairbrush. Handle foliage with great care when cleaning it.

Plants whose stems have become elongated and leggy with sparse growth should be cut back to maintain a uniform appearance. If growth is sparse along the entire stem, pinch it off at its junction with the main stem or at soil level if the leggy stem emanates directly from the root system. If growth is sparse only along the section of stem that protrudes beyond the rest of the plant, pinch it back enough to eliminate the protrusion.

Keep withered foliage removed. It is not uncom-

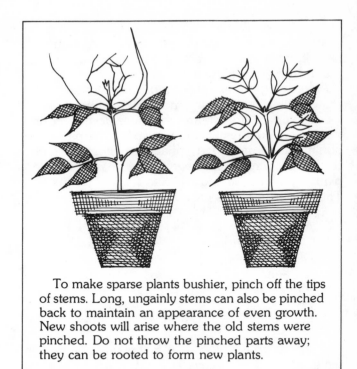

To make sparse plants bushier, pinch off the tips of stems. Long, ungainly stems can also be pinched back to maintain an appearance of even growth. New shoots will arise where the old stems were pinched. Do not throw the pinched parts away; they can be rooted to form new plants.

mon for a few old leaves to die now and then since plants are not immortal. Such routine pruning is not unlike trimming our hair.

Faded flowers should be removed as soon as they are spent. Otherwise, the flowers will produce seed. If the plant is not allowed to mature its seed, it will continue to produce flowers in its attempt to produce seed. If too many seeds are allowed to mature,

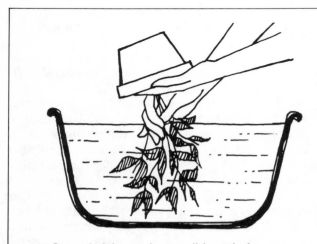

Smooth foliage plants will benefit from an occasional bath in tepid, soapy water to remove grime or insects.

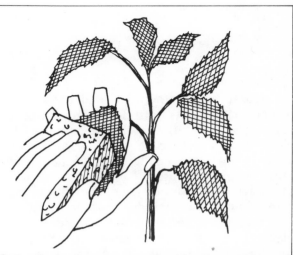

Wiping the leaves once a week with a damp sponge also helps to keep plants looking their best.

the plant has completed its life cycle. Many flowering plants may then die. Pinching off faded flowers also stimulates branching, bud formation, and therefore a bushier plant with more flowers.

Give all your plants a half turn every 2 or 3 weeks. The side of the plant which receives more light is generally a little perkier than the darker side. This is especially true of plants that are in windows. Turning plants periodically to distribute light evenly gives them a more uniform and healthy appearance.

Locating plants outdoors for the summer

The indoor environment is an unnatural one for all plants. Though many can be grown quite successfully inside, all will benefit from being placed outdoors during the warm summer months. Fresh air, filtered sunlight, and rainwater all have a rejuvenating effect on house plants.

Relocate the plants gradually, placing them outdoors in a shady spot for a few hours each day, then bringing them back indoors at night. After 4 or 5 days of this treatment, they will be acclimatized to the outdoor environment and can be left out both day and night until a few weeks before the first anticipated frost. This process of gradual transition is called *hardening*. An abrupt change of environment is always traumatic for house plants, but hardening them gradually makes the transition easier and greatly reduces the chances of injuring the plants.

Locate the plants outside either with their containers exposed or buried in the ground. Plunging the containers into the ground up to the rims will reduce their watering needs.

Select a shaded spot beside a row of shrubbery or under a tree. Dig a trench deep enough to accomodate the entire pot and fill the bottom with sand or gravel to assure good drainage. Set the plants so

Locate your plants outdoors for the summer; the fresh air and rainwater will do them good.

that the rims of the containers are even with or slightly below the level of the surrounding soil. Fill in around them with soil and apply 1 or 2 inches of mulch around the stems of the plants to conserve moisture and reduce the need for watering. Mulching also prevents rain from splashing soil onto the foliage and thereby reduces the spread of diseases. During times of sparse rainfall, water your plants as you would if they were indoors. Do not expose plants to drying winds or to direct sunlight, especially in areas where summers are particularly warm.

The outdoor summer treatment is especially recommended for plants that have begun to look a little haggard indoors. Once plants are established in their outdoor environment, fertilize them with a mild liquid fertilizer solution. Plants will produce considerable growth during the summer. About a month before bringing plants back indoors, however, withhold fertilizer until the plants have readjusted to the indoors.

Keep a close eye on your house plants while they are outdoors. They will be exposed to many of the insects that attack outdoor plants. When insects or signs of disease are detected, take immediate action to control them (see *Curing Plant Ailments*).

Move plants indoors before the first frost threatens in the fall. Make the move indoors as gradual as the move outdoors, bringing the plants inside for a few hours each day before leaving them there for the winter. Once the plants have readjusted to their indoor environment, repot those that have become too crowded in their containers. You may prefer to repot them before bringing them indoors. Be certain that plants are free of insect pests before bringing them back in.

Shape leggy plants by pinching back overgrown shoots. Resume regular watering and withhold fertilizer until late winter.

Vacation care for house plants

Before leaving town on vacation, make arrangements with a friend or neighbor to water your house plants while you are away. If this is not possible, the following precautions will help your plants survive in your absence.

If you vacation during the summer, plunge the plants in the soil outdoors, burying the pots up to their rims (see *Locating Plants Outdoors for the Summer*). If you vacation during the cooler months or if you do not move your plants outside for the summer, water each plant thoroughly, let it drain, and place the pot inside a plastic bag, leaving the plant itself uncovered. Tie the bag loosely around the base of the stem, but do not seal it completely. This allows some air to penetrate the soil surface and get into the root zone. Place the bagged pot in a cool, shaded spot. The soil moisture should be adequate for the plant for several weeks.

Moving house plants long distances

If you must relocate to a new home in another city or state, the care you exercise in preparing your plants for the move will determine their ability to survive.

Water the plants thoroughly then cover them with plastic bags to retain as much moisture as possible. Small plants can be covered with sandwich bags or cellophane. Cover large plants with bags such as those used to cover garments coming back from the dry cleaner. Large, sprawling plants, such as saddle leaf philodendron (*P. selloum*), will require particular care. Gather the stems together in an upright position and secure them by looping a strip of soft cloth around them, then cover the plant with a dry cleaning bag. Plants in hanging containers should be covered with plastic and, if possible, situated in the moving vehicle where they can hang. Secure all plastic covering below the rim of the pot to assure moisture retention.

Most house plants can survive without light for 2 or 3 days if they have adequate moisture. Beyond 3 days, however, recovery from the trip becomes increasingly difficult. If it is at all possible, transport plants in a car or other vehicle in which they may receive light. If plants must be moved in a closed vehicle, check them each day of the trip. The plants will enjoy a breath of fresh air and whatever light you can give them. Avoid extreme temperatures, either too hot or too cold.

Displaying House Plants

Plants can transform an entire room in one day from a lifeless, dry environment (no matter how elegant the decor) to a living, natural environment. Plants can make a large, bare room smaller and more intimate, and a small room seem airy, less closed in.

Well-grown plants can create an atmosphere of warmth in almost any indoor situation. Although decorating ideas will come primarily from your own imagination, a few hints will perhaps help. First, is the plant you wish to display fit for display? Is it healthy? Do you like the container in which it is potted? The variety of containers available is vast enough that you need never settle for a container you don't like, or one that does not blend with the room in which you locate it. Finally, do the plant and the container harmonize?

The size and texture of the plants you select must complement the surroundings in which you place them. Large, coarse textured plants often seem cumbersome and out of place in a small room. Look around the room you wish to decorate and let your eye wander to the voids in wall or floor space that could be filled with plants. Make a mental note of the size of the area and keep it in mind when you are in a plant store. A mature loquat or weeping fig can fill a large void if you have a bare wall, and a small maidenhair fern is a delicate and alluring filler on an end table or narrow sill. A staghorn fern mounted on a sphagnum moss wall plaque or a

half-rounded hanging basket makes an excellent alternative to framed art and other wall decor.

The next question to ask yourself is which plants will grow in the location you have in mind? Factors to consider include light, temperature, humidity, and air circulation. Remember that you must avoid placing plants near heating outlets, fireplaces, drafty windows, and other places that cause severe temperature fluctuation. Don't be afraid to try a particular plant in any location, provided the growing conditions seem right.

You can, however, exercise a great deal of control over the growing environment of plants. By using fluorescent lights (see Chapter Two, *Using Artificial Lighting*), you can grow plants in a room that receives very little sunlight. You can raise humidity in dry places (see Chapter Two, *Temperature and Humidity*) and often find a temperature variation of up to 5° in one room.

The following large plants are useful in floor planters or on low tables and stands. Recommended light conditions are indicated by B (bright), M (medium), or L (low):

Dracaena	L–M
Elephant-foot tree	B
Fig, weeping	M–B
Japanese aralia	M–B
Kentia palm	L
Laurel, Sweet Bay	B
Loquat	B
Monstera	L–M
Norfolk Island pine	L–M
Philodendron *(P. selloum)*	L–M
Schefflera	M–B
Sentry palm	M

The selection of decorative containers is unending.

A floor planter by a window.

The following small plants are good fillers where space is tight but spotted with small gaps. Small plants are also suited to narrow shelves or window sills. Here are some favorite small plants recommended for beginners:

African violet	B
Aloe, Burn plant	M–B
Artillery plant	M
Echeveria	M–B
Golden ball cactus	B
Hen-and-chickens	M–B
Living stones	B
Maidenhair fern	M
Peperomia	M
Piggyback plant	M
Prayer plant, Maranta	M

Some of these will not stay small forever, but are useful for filling small places while they are young. Move them as it becomes necessary, both to provide growing room for the plant and to add variety to the indoor garden scene.

Medium-size plants are effective in both large and small rooms. Choose the plant that will look best in the growing conditions provided by each location you have in mind.

Bathrooms and kitchens deserve special mention because these are more humid than other rooms. However, kitchens are usually brightly lighted whereas bathrooms often receive low light. Place humidity-loving plants near sinks and bath tubs.

Large plants can be dramatic as single specimens, but most plants are best displayed in groups. The two keys to grouping plants are compatibility of size and leaf texture and similarity of cultural requirements. Different species of ferns work well together, as do groups of cacti, succulents, or bromeliads.

Some genera, such as *Coleus* or *Begonia,* are so large that it is not difficult to find 4 or 5 plants within the genus that are varied in appearance but similar in cultural requirements. Groups such as philodendron, dracaena, dieffenbachia, azalea, and palms all contain several commonly available species that require similar light, temperature, humidity, soil, moisture, and fertility. In grouping plants, the containers should, of course, also complement each other. To summarize briefly, house plants are more pleasing to the eye in groups than they are scattered about. They are also easier to care for.

Vining plants can be displayed in a number of ways. Locate them on shelves where they can trail or in hanging baskets from which they will cascade (see Chapter Six, *Indoor Hanging Gardens*), or provide support, such as a moss stick, and watch them climb.

A floor planter by a sunny stairwell.

House plants are wonderful problem solvers for the interior decorator, both amateur and professional. Plants can fill empty corners and awkward gaps, fill blank walls, or accent sculpture and framed art. A window garden or hanging basket makes an enticing display, and a well-grown plant is always a good choice for a centerpiece on the kitchen or dining room table.

To keep plants looking their best, remove dead or sick-looking stems and leaves whenever you see them. Remove unhealthy plants from the display groups so that they won't detract from the rest of the display. Once the plant has recovered, replace it in the group. If growth problems recur, you have probably located the plant in a place not suited to its cultural needs. You may have to try the plant in a half dozen locations before you find the one in which it will thrive. Don't hesitate to move a plant that isn't doing well; the experimentation is half the fun.

The bathroom is an excellent location for plants whose humidity requirements are high.

Modern homes lend themselves particularly well to displaying house plants along a wall.

Plants for the living room include Chinese evergreens on the left, bamboo palm behind the chair, and a young weeping fig on the right.

Curing Plant Ailments

House plants are not without their problems. The difficult growing environment found in most homes puts plants at a disadvantage from the day they are brought in the door. Happily, these problems are not insurmountable. Constant vigilance and immediate action can restore distressed plants to health and vigor.

Plants are susceptible to a number of difficulties. Improper light, soil moisture, humidity, or temperature can all cause damage. In addition, several insect pests commonly vex house plants. Aphids, scale insects, and whiteflies secrete a sticky, milky substance that encourages the growth of sooty mold fungus. Failure to sterilize soil in which tender young plants are potted may result in their loss to the fungus disease called *damping-off*.

When troubles occur, act immediately to cure them, but don't overreact. Often enough, problems can be overcome simply by relocating a plant or by withholding water for a day or two. Here are some common problems, their symptoms, and their cures:

Yellowing of lower leaves. Newly purchased plants, shocked by a new environment, sometimes shed lower leaves. If leaf drop is accompanied by softening of the lower stems and a tendency of the soil to stay soggy, the problem may be too much water or poor drainage in the container. Withhold water for 2 or 3 days to see if the soil dries out. If it does not, repot the plant in a more porous soil mix and fill the bottom of the container with pebbles to improve drainage. Overwatered cacti become mushy.

Wilting or curling of leaf edges. This could be caused by too little water, too much heat, too much fertilizer, too little humidity, or a combination of all these. Damaged leaves may become brittle, develop brown spots, and fall off. Avoid placing plants near radiators or other heating outlets. If watering doesn't restore health, mist the foliage daily. Humidity can be raised by placing pots on a shallow tray of pebbles filled nearly to the top of the pebbles with water. Underwatered cacti and succulents may become pale or begin to yellow.

Brown or yellow spots on leaves are usually caused by too much light. Move the plant to a location where sunlight is not as bright. If you are using artificial lighting, move the plants farther away from the lights. If spots persist, a fungus disease may be the cause. Apply daconil or maneb according to label instructions.

Long, spindly stems and pale leaves. Plants tend to lean toward their source of light. If lighting is insufficient, the plants must "stretch," resulting in weak, spindly growth. Leaves may pale or appear stunted. Give afflicted plants a brighter location. If you are using artificial lighting, move the plants nearer to the lamps. When normal growth resumes, pinch back leggy growth so that it is in proportion to the rest of the plant.

Tips of leaves turn brown. If leaves and stems are broken or bent, discoloration of the tips of the leaves may be the result of bruising. Ferns are particularly sensitive to bruising. Move plants to a location where they are less likely to be brushed against. Trim off damaged parts with scissors.

Top leaves are stunted. If the plant produces rapid growth that never seems to mature, it may have received too much soluble fertilizer in one dose, thus the rest of the fertilizer that the plant was unable to use so rapidly, drained through the soil. Therefore, the new growth is left with nothing to sustain it. Give the plant more light, less fertilizer, and scrape off salts that have formed on the soil or on the pots (see Chapter Two, *Fertilizing House Plants*). Then water thoroughly to leach out excess salts.

Leaves turn dull green to yellow and bottom leaves drop. New leaves, if there are any at all, are stunted and weak. These are symptoms of nutrient deficiency. Fertilize plants more frequently, especially during the growing seasons of spring, summer, and early fall.

Sudden dropping of leaves; leaves turn yellow. These symptoms could be caused by a sudden change in temperature. Some plants are especially sensitive to drafts and to temperature changes of as little as 5°. Plants brought home during winter, especially where winters are severe, may experience this sort of trauma. If the plant continues to lose leaves, check the roots to be certain they haven't rotted. If the roots are healthy, prune them back a little to renew vigor, and repot the plant. Be certain to keep plants away from radiators and out of drafts.

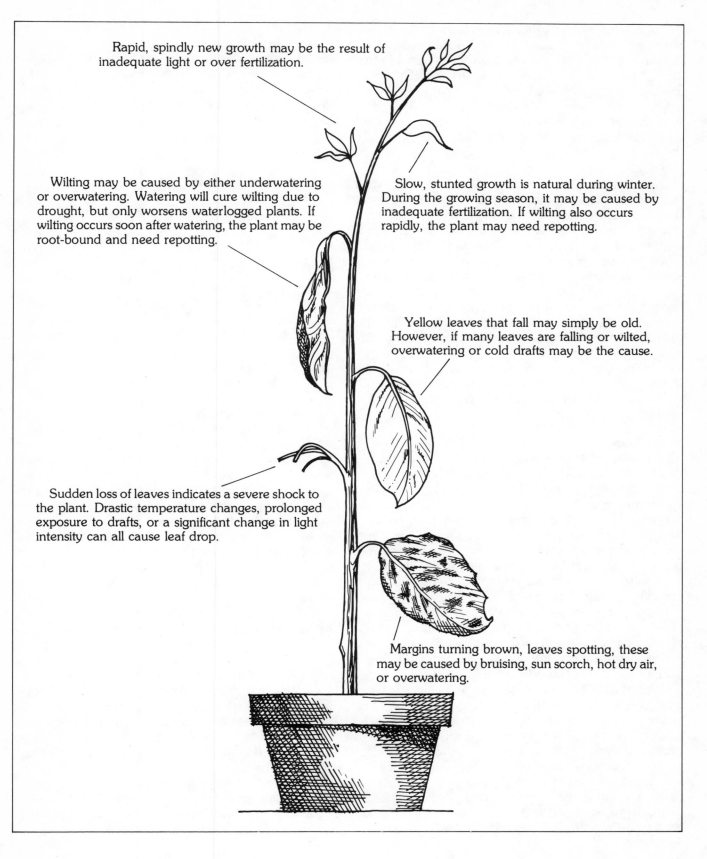

Rapid, spindly new growth may be the result of inadequate light or over fertilization.

Wilting may be caused by either underwatering or overwatering. Watering will cure wilting due to drought, but only worsens waterlogged plants. If wilting occurs soon after watering, the plant may be root-bound and need repotting.

Slow, stunted growth is natural during winter. During the growing season, it may be caused by inadequate fertilization. If wilting also occurs rapidly, the plant may need repotting.

Yellow leaves that fall may simply be old. However, if many leaves are falling or wilted, overwatering or cold drafts may be the cause.

Sudden loss of leaves indicates a severe shock to the plant. Drastic temperature changes, prolonged exposure to drafts, or a significant change in light intensity can all cause leaf drop.

Margins turning brown, leaves spotting, these may be caused by bruising, sun scorch, hot dry air, or overwatering.

Pot-bound plants; roots growing through drainage hole. Roots of overcrowded plants may also appear on the surface. Small and medium plants should be repotted when this occurs (see Chapter Two, *Repotting House Plants.*) If plants are too large to easily repot, loosen the surface soil and remove the top 2 inches. Add fresh soil to replace what you have removed. This is called *top-dressing* the plant.

Knotted roots. If stunted growth causes you to suspect the plant needs repotting and you discover that the roots are knotted and twisted, your problem may be *nematodes.* These microscopic creatures are often present in garden soil. For this reason, potting soil should always be sterilized (see Chapter Two, *Soil For House Plants*). Prune off damaged roots and gently wash the old soil off the healthy roots. Repot the plant in sterilized potting soil and drench the soil with a nematocide, such as *Nemagon* or *Fumazone.* Sterilizing your potting soils will also help to avert fungus diseases.

If you must remove roots, remove a portion of the top growth, too, to aid the roots in recovering. Root these cuttings to propagate new plants in case nematode control on the mother plant is not possible.

Insect pests

A number of insect pests may attack house plants. Always inspect plants carefully before buying to be certain the plants are free from insects and diseases. Plants that have been outside during the summer should be very closely inspected before they are brought back in. Cut flowers and other garden greenery for indoor decoration may also harbor insects. Discard infested plants immediately; pretty as the flowers may be, they are not worth the woes of trying to rid house plants of insect pests.

Should you discover infestation on a house plant, segregate it immediately. Then inspect all your plants closely and segregate those with insects, no matter how minor the infestation may appear. Some insects can reproduce with incredible speed.

If infestation is light, washing the foliage with a mild solution of household detergent and warm water (2 teaspoons detergent to a gallon of water) may be all that's required to control insects on foliage plants. Smooth, broadleaf plants such as rubber plants, dieffenbachia, dracaena, Chinese evergreen, and snake plant (*Sansevieria*) should receive a regular monthly washing. Keep infested plants segregated and watch them closely for a few days to be certain the infestation is under control.

If infestation is severe, it may be necessary to use insecticides to rid plants of insect pests. Most insecticides have offensive odors and should be applied outside or in an area such as a basement or a garage where the odor will not be a problem. The following descriptions will help you to identify insect pests and to select proper control methods:

A good spraying with the sink hose can remove light infestations of many insects.

Aphids are small green, pink, red, or black insects that cluster on the undersides of leaves or on stems and flowerbuds. Common aphids are $1/16$ to $1/8$ inch long and have rounded or pear-shaped bodies with long legs and antennae. Some aphids appear woolly because of a waxy covering. These insects suck juices from plants, causing poor, stunted growth and curled or distorted leaves. Aphids secrete a sticky honeydew which is attractive to ants. Control aphids by hand-picking them off, by washing foliage, by swabbing with alcohol, or, if infestation is severe, by spraying with malathion or diazinon.

Caterpillars and cutworms may reach $1\frac{1}{2}$ to 2 inches at maturity and are either striped, mottled, or solid brown, red, yellow, gray, green, or black. Some are covered with dense hair. Cutworms usually hide in the soil or deep within flowers and are therefore difficult to detect. Leaves, buds, or flowers that are partly eaten may be evidence of cutworms and other caterpillars. Handpick caterpillars that you do see. If damage continues or worsens, spray plants and drench soil with malathion or diazinon.

Cyclamen mites are too small to see without the aid of a magnifying glass. Under a glass, they appear as oval, tan, semitransparent glistening mites. Their eggs are oval and pearly white. Mites spread by crawling from plant to plant where leaves touch.

Ivies and African violets are especially susceptible to attack. Infested ivy may have deformed leaves or no leaves at all. Leaves of African violets become twisted and excessively hairy. Buds may be deformed and fail to open. Flowers are deformed and streaked. Remove damaged parts of plants and destroy them. Control cyclamen mites by spraying with dicofol (Kelthane). Make 2 or 3 applications at 10-day intervals.

Fungus gnats are flylike insects about ⅛ inch long. Immature forms, called maggots, are attracted to soil that is high in decaying organic matter. Maggots burrow in the soil, feeding on plant roots. Infested plants make slow growth, appear off-color, and may lose foliage. Control maggots by drenching soil with rotenone. Adult gnats cause no damage but are a nuisance. They are repelled by sprays containing rotenone.

Mealybugs are small, soft-bodied insects that look like tiny pieces of cotton because of their waxy covering. Mature insects may be 1/16 inch long. Mealybugs are found on stems, axils (junction of leaf and stem), or undersides of leaves. They lay their eggs in clusters that are enclosed in white, cottony material. The ground mealybug or root mealybug lives in the soil and feeds on roots of African violets and other plants. Mealybugs suck plant juices, stunting plant growth or killing the plant. The ground mealybug damages plant rootlets, causing plants to grow slowly and to wilt rapidly after watering. Wash the plants with soapy water to control light infestations of mealybugs. If infestation becomes severe, spray plants and drench soil with malathion. Always segregate infested plants until insect populations have disappeared.

Millipedes are wormlike creatures with many short legs arranged along the body. The hard bodies are brown, tan, or gray and may grow to 1½ inches long. Millipedes hide under containers and boards and are most numerous in moist places where there is organic matter to feed on. They are most active at night and tend to assume a coil form when disturbed. Millipedes feed on seeds, roots, and lower stems and become a nuisance when present in large numbers. A tidy growing area, free from organic debris, will discourage the presence of millipedes. Destroy occasional millipedes by hand-picking. If millipedes become a problem, drench hiding places with rotenone spray.

Psocids (bark lice) are small, pale yellowish-white to gray insects that grow to ¹/₃₂ or ¹/₁₆ inch long. They may cluster in numbers of 100 or more to feed on dead animal or vegetable matter. Though damage done to house plants by psocids is questionable, large numbers are a nuisance. Control psocids by spraying soil, containers, saucers, and shelves with rotenone. If psocids do attack the top of the plant, control them with malathion or diazinon.

Scale insects are common house plant pests. Most species are ¹/₁₆ to ⅛ inch in diameter and have a shell-like covering. Most are brown, gray, or white. Scale insects lay eggs in a whitish sac secreted from under the shell. These clusters can be mistaken for mealybugs, so examine the infestation closely to detect the shells that are characteristic of scale insects. Scale insects suck plant juices from leaves and stems, leaving a sticky liquid called *honeydew* which attracts ants. Honeydew also provides a base for the growth of sooty mold, a fungus disease. Malathion, in solution with household detergent, controls scale insects. Use ½ teaspoon detergent to 1 gallon malathion spray solution. If the first application does not bring complete control, make weekly applications until control is complete.

Sowbugs, or pillbugs, have oval, segmented, shell-like bodies ¼ to ½ inch long. Most species are gray or brown. These insects like humid places. They are most active at night and hide under loose soil or other cover during the day. Sowbugs feed on decaying organic matter and plant roots. Spray pots, soil, and other hiding places with rotenone to control them.

Spider mites, also called *red spiders*, are tiny red, green, or yellow mites that cling to the undersides of leaves and suck plant juices. When numerous, spider mites form a silky webbing on leaves and stems. Early symptoms of damage by spider mites include speckled areas on leaves, and, as the situation worsens, whole leaves may become yellow and drop off the plant. Seriously infested plants become stunted and may even die. Segregate infested plants immediately, then spray them with malathion or dicofol (Kelthane). Be certain to spray both top and bottom leaf surfaces. It may take several weekly applications to fully control spider mites since numerous eggs may hatch during this period.

Thrips are tiny tan, brown, or black insects that are barely visible to the naked eye. The young may be yellow or orange. Thrips suck juices from leaves and flowers. Injury appears as irregular or streaked silvered areas that are speckled with black dots. Foliage may be blotched and fall off, and flowers may be streaked or otherwise distorted. To control thrips, spray plants with malathion or diazinon.

Whiteflies are about ¹/₁₆ inch long and have white, wedge-shaped wings. Whiteflies swarm about a plant where they are harboring if the plant is moved. Both tops and undersides of leaves are targets for whiteflies. Whiteflies suck juices from leaves of plants, causing leaves to become pale, turn yellow, and drop off. Leaves become covered with sticky *honeydew* which attracts ants and supports the growth of sooty mold. Segregate infested plants immediately and spray them at weekly intervals with rotenone, malathion, or diazinon, until control of whiteflies is complete.

Diseases

Though house plants are less prone to diseases than outdoor plants, they are not immune. The following table lists some common house plant diseases and their remedies:

Symptoms	Disease	Plant	Control Suggestions
Seedlings turn dark at soil level, rot, and fall over.	Damping-off	Seedlings of most flowers and house plants	Use sterilized soil; dust seed or plant roots; dust surface of soil; drench soil using Captan, 1½ tablespoons per gallon of water, or Terraclor, 1 tablespoon per gallon of water.
White powdery growth on surface of leaves, buds, and stems.	Mildew	Most leafy ornamentals	Provide better ventilation; avoid sprinkling plants; spray with Karathane, ½ teaspoon per gallon of water, or Benlate, 1–2 teaspoons per gallon of water.
A corky scab, light brown, usually on underside of leaves and along stems. Often occurs during late winter.	Dropsy (Odema)		Do not water excessively, especially during cloudy weather.
Plants stunted and sickly, swellings on plant roots.	Nematodes	Most house plants	Make new leaf cuttings in peat or vermiculite; plant in sterilized soil; discard infested plants.
Plants sickly, wilting; brown soft rot on crowns and leaf stems.	Crown rot and root rot	African violet	Avoid overwatering; drench soil with Captan, ½ tablespoon per gallon of water. Destroy badly diseased plants. Do not take cuttings from diseased plants.
Soft, tan-colored rot of crowns, buds, flowers, and leaf stems. A tannish-brown growth may cover the surface of leaves.	Botrytis blight (Gray mold)		Increase air circulation; avoid sprinkling foliage; spray with Captan, 1½ tablespoons per gallon of water.
Leaves yellowish, scorched at margins and tips.	Leaf scorch		Shade plants from bright sun.

Symptoms	Disease	Plant	Control suggestions
Plants dwarfed with crinkled leaves; leaves mottled light and dark green.	Mosaic	African violet	Destroy infected plants; start new virus-free plants.
Small circular tan or bleached spots on leaves.	Leaf spot		Do not place plants in sunlight until the leaves are dry.
Leaves turn brown, wither, and fall.	Leaf drop	Asparagus fern	Room temperature too high: lower to 68° to 70°; increase humidity.
Enlarged areas or galls on roots.	Root knot		Divide plants, separating healthy roots with tops; plant in sterilized soil; discard infested parts.
Soft, tan-colored rot of crowns, buds, flowers, and leaf stems. A tannish-brown growth may cover the surface of leaves.	Botrytis blight (Gray mold)	Begonia	Increase air circulation; avoid sprinkling foliage; spray with Zineb or Captan, 1½ tablespoons per gallon of water.
Stems and crowns water-soaked and darkened at soil level; stems collapse and die.	Stem, crown, and root rot		Discard infected plants; drench soil with Captan or Zineb, 1½ tablespoons per gallon of water or Terraclor, 1–2 teaspoons per gallon of water.
Large, round galls on stems and roots.	Crown gall		Make tip cuttings in sterilized soil; destroy infected plants.
Swellings on roots.	Root knot		Make new leaf cuttings in peat or vermiculite; plant in sterilized soil; discard infested plants.
Roots and base of plants turn soft and rot.	Root rot	Cactus	Repot in sterilized soil; water sparingly and uniformly.
Irregular rust or corky spots, usually on older stems. Severe attacks may reduce flowering and kill plant.	Corky scab		Usually may be checked by increasing the light and decreasing the humidity.
Soft, slimy decayed tuber.	Tuber rot	Caladium	Use disease-free tubers and plant in sterilized soil. Provide good ventilation and do not overwater.

Symptoms	Disease	Plant	Control Suggestions
Dead areas on leaves; restricted brown spots.	Anthracnose	Chinese evergreen (Philodendron, Dieffenbachia, Aglaonema)	Avoid chilling; don't sprinkle leaves; spray with Zineb, 1½ tablespoons per gallon of water.
Seedlings or cuttings wilt and rot; may be a blackening at base of stem.	Damping-off	Coleus	Destroy diseased plants. Start seedlings and cuttings in sterilized soil.
Soft, tan-colored rot of crowns, leaves, and stems. A tannish-brown growth may cover the surface of leaves.	Botrytis blight (Gray mold)	Ferns	Increase air circulation; avoid sprinkling foliage; spray with Zineb, or Captan, 1½ tablespoons per gallon of water.
Galls are not a sign of disease but rather are natural spore producing receptacles.	Brown leaf galls		
Spots appear light green and water soaked, turning brown or black; margin of spot reddish.	Bacterial leaf spot and stem canker	English ivy	Avoid high temperatures, moist conditions, and unnecessary syringing. Water plants from below.
Roots and stems decayed.	Stem and root rot	Fuchsia	Use sterilized soil for starting new plants.
Leaves yellow and sickly; veins remain green.	Chlorosis	Gardenia	Caused by iron deficiency; treat with Sequestrene at manufacturer's direction, or add pinch of iron sulfate to soil.
Buds fall from plants.	Bud drop		Avoid chilling and sudden change of temperature; keep humidity high.
Swellings on roots.	Root knot		Make new leaf cuttings in peat or vermiculite; plant in sterilized soil; discard infested plants.
Sunken, discolored areas on stems at soil level; wilting, yellowing, and falling of leaves.	Stem canker		Avoid overwatering and poor drainage; drench soil with Bordeaux mixture or other copper fungicide.

Symptoms	Disease	Plant	Control Suggestions
Soft tan-colored rot of crowns, buds, flowers, and leaf stems. A tannish-brown growth may cover the surface of the leaves.	Botrytis blight (Gray mold)	Geranium	Increase air circulation; avoid sprinkling foliage; spray with Zineb or Captan, 1½ tablespoons per gallon of water.
Soft, dark, slimy rot at soil level.	Stem rot		Make new leaf cuttings; plant in sterilized soil; destroy diseased plants.
Water-soaked spots on leaves later turning corky; corky ridges on leaf stems.	Dropsy (Odema)		Avoid high soil moisture; provide better light and ventilation.
Disfigured leaves with striking concentric zonal spots. Plant may be stunted.	Ring spot	Peperomia	Make new cuttings from healthy leaves; plant in sterilized soil; discard infected plants.
Leaves turn yellow and fall.	Chlorosis	Poinsettia	Avoid chilling and overwatering; provide adequate lighting.
Long water-soaked streaks on one side of green stems.	Bacterial canker		Make new cuttings and plant in sterilized soil; avoid overhead watering; destroy infected plants.
Lower portions of stem turn black and decay.	Stem rot		Start new cuttings from disease-free plants in sterilized sand; drench soil with mixture of 1 tablespoon Terraclor plus 1½ tablespoons Captan per gallon of water.
Dark colored, restricted spots on leaves; dead tissue later dries and falls out.	Anthracnose	Rubber plant	Spray with Zineb, 1½ tablespoons per gallon of water.
Leaves turn yellow, scorched at margins and tips.	Leaf scorch		Reduce the amount of direct sunlight; increase humidity. Plants should be hardened off before leaving greenhouse.
Blighting of foliage.	Blight	German ivy	Reduce humidity by spacing plants; spray with Captan or Zineb, 1½ tablespoons per gallon of water.

Propagating House Plants

To increase the number of plants in your home you may wish to propagate your plants. Propagating means helping the plants to reproduce. Many plants can be propagated by cutting off a stem or leaf and placing it in water to form new roots, a process called "rooting." Not all cuttings will form roots in water. Many will have to be rooted in sand or in a mixture of peat moss and perlite, both of which are available at garden supply stores. After the new plants have formed roots, you will have to plant them in containers. Ordinary garden loam will suffice for a number of plants, or you can obtain sterilized potting soil from the garden supply store. In addition, you will need a sharp knife or pair of scissors to make the cuttings.

There are no great tricks to propagating house plants. It is a natural response in the plant, a survival mechanism, to form roots where cuts have been made. Provide a small container with rooting medium and nature does the rest. Make cuts as cleanly as possible.

Other methods of propagating house plants include seeds, runners and offsets, and air-layering. The simplest method of propagation consists of dividing the root ball of a plant to form 2 or more plants.

The instructions which follow will help you to increase your plants, either for use in your home or to give as gifts. The directions for each method of propagation are followed by a list of plants best propagated by that method.

Seeds

Few house plants are commonly grown from seed. Florist plants such as primrose, cyclamen, sultana, and begonia are exceptions. Because so few house plants are grown from seed, seeds may be difficult to obtain. Furthermore, if you want only 2 or 3 plants of a given species, propagation from seed is impractical. A better method of propagating only a few plants is to root cuttings taken from a healthy plant. If, however, you should wish to grow a great number of plants, either for yourself or to give as gifts, sowing seeds is probably the least expensive and least time-consuming method of propagation. Get an early start with gift plants; many foliage plants require up to a year to develop as attractive specimens.

The following plants are among the easiest to propagate from seed:

- Agave
- Asparagus fern
- Avocado
- Bromeliads
- Cactus
- Citrus (grapefruit, lemon, orange)
- Coleus
- Gloxinia
- Impatiens
- Kalanchoe
- Monstera
- Norfolk Island pine
- Phoenix (date palm)
- Schefflera

Many outdoor garden plants can be grown from seed indoors. Fill a pot with potting soil (equal parts loam, peat moss, and perlite or sand) and sow seed according to the instructions on the seed packets. Most will need a sunny location for optimum flower production. The following annuals and perennials respond well to indoor culture:

- Alyssum
- Begonia
- Black-eyed Susan vine
- Campanula
- Chrysanthemum
- Geranium
- Hepatica
- Hibiscus
- Marigold
- Morning glory
- Nicotiana
- Petunia
- Phlox
- Pinks (*Dianthus*)
- Portulaca
- Torenia
- Verbena
- Zinnia

In addition to these, many members of the succulent family can also be grown from seed.

Sow seeds in flats and pot seedlings later, or sow seeds directly in pots. In either case, a standard potting mixture of 1 part garden loam, 1 part peat moss or finely ground compost, and 1 part sand or perlite will produce satisfactory results for most plants. To assure healthy seedlings, it is advisable to sterilize soil before planting seeds (see Chapter Two, *Soil for House Plants*). You can also purchase sterilized potting soil at the garden supply store. Scrub pots clean and sterilize them, too. Sterilize clay pots in the oven along with the soil. Plastic containers and others that cannot be placed in the oven can be sterilized by dipping them in a solution of 1 part household bleach to 9 parts water.

Place a 1-inch layer of gravel in the bottom of the pot to provide good drainage. Fill the pot with sterilized soil to within 1 inch of the rim and firm it with the heel of your hand. Sprinkle seeds over the surface and cover them evenly with ⅛ to ¼ inch of sphagnum moss or finely ground compost. If seed is especially small, place seed on top of the layer of sphagnum moss rather than under it.

Place pots of seeds in a saucer of lukewarm water. The water will be drawn up through the drainage hole until the medium is moist all the way to the surface. Watering containers of seeds from the top may wash the seeds too far down into the medium, retarding or completely preventing successful germination. If you sow seeds in flats, place the planted

To sow seeds in a pot, place a layer of pebbles or gravel in the bottom of the pot to assure good drainage; then fill the pot with soil to 1 inch below the rim. Sprinkle seeds on the surface. Press large seeds into the soil to a depth twice their diameter. Cover small seeds with ⅛ to ¼ inch of soil and firm it with the bottom of a dry pot. To keep the soil evenly moist without disturbing the surface, water seeded pots from the bottom or double-pot them.

flat in a tray of water until the soil is moist throughout, then remove to a shady, warm, humid location. Place plastic bags over pots to retain humidity. Cover flats with cellophane or polyethylene plastic.

As seedlings begin to sprout, poke ventilation holes in the plastic. Then two weeks later remove the plastic covering. Keep soil moist but never soaked. When seedlings develop the second set of leaves, pot them in individual containers.

Stem cuttings

A number of house plants are propagated from stem cuttings. A stem cutting is a 2- to 4-inch section of stem or branch with 2 or more nodes (spots on the stem from which leaves arise). Do not take cuttings of stems that are too flexible; these may be too young and may wilt before they can form roots. Use a sharp knife or scissors to make cuttings.

Use a pot or small flat as a rooting bed. Common rooting media include a mixture of equal parts perlite and vermiculite, or sharp sand. Sharp sand is coarse and grainy and permits air to circulate in the area of the cutting where roots will form. Cover the drainage hole in the pot with moss or other material to keep the rooting medium from running out. Fill the pot with the rooting medium and firm it with your hand. Moisten to settle it; then poke holes in the medium with a pencil to facilitate inserting the cuttings.

Remove all but the top 3 or 4 leaves from the cutting. Insert it ½ to ⅔ of its length in the medium and water again to settle the medium around the cutting. Place an inverted jar over the pot, if you have one large enough, or cover the bed with clear plastic to retain humidity. Place cuttings in a warm, bright location that will not receive direct sunlight. A north or east window is often good. Water the cuttings from the bottom as you do pots or flats of seeds. Cuttings may wilt if temperatures are too high or sun is too bright. A temperature range of 65 to 70 degrees should promote successful rooting for most cuttings.

Some cuttings will root fairly quickly. Coleus, for instance, may form roots in only 7 to 10 days. Other plants may require 1 to 4 weeks. Do not be impatient with your cuttings unless they begin to wilt and a change of location does not revive them. Signs of new growth on the cuttings indicate that rooting is taking place.

Tug gently at plants you suspect may have

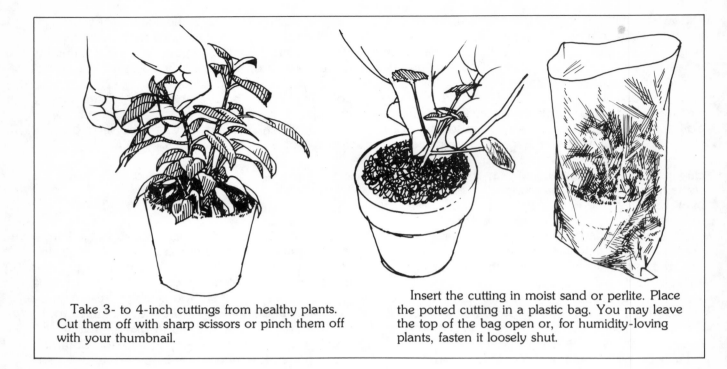

Take 3- to 4-inch cuttings from healthy plants. Cut them off with sharp scissors or pinch them off with your thumbnail.

Insert the cutting in moist sand or perlite. Place the potted cutting in a plastic bag. You may leave the top of the bag open or, for humidity-loving plants, fasten it loosely shut.

rooted. Those plants that do not readily pull out of the rooting medium have formed roots and are ready to be potted individually.

Plants that generally respond well to propagation by stem cuttings include the following:

    Aluminum plant
    Artillery plant
    Begonia
    Christmas cactus
    Coleus
    Croton
    Crown-of-thorns
    Dieffenbachia (cuttings from main stem)
    Dracaena
    Echeveria
    Fittonia
    Impatiens
    Ivies
    Jade plant
    Kalanchoe
    Monstera
    Nephthytis
    Old man cactus
    Osmanthus
    Peperomia
    Philodendron
    Poinsettia (tips of new growth)
    Rubber plant
    Wandering Jew

Leaf cuttings

Plants with thick petioles (leaf stems) or thick, juicy leaves (succulents) may be propagated by leaf cuttings. Make cuttings of a whole leaf or part of a leaf. Insert these in sand or other rooting medium to form roots. (Some plants will form tiny plantlets at the base of the cutting.)

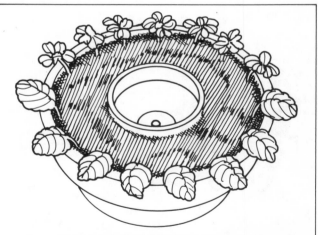

A small clay pot placed inside a larger pot serves as a reservoir, seeping water slowly into the rooting medium in which the cuttings are placed. Plug the drainage hole of the inside pot and keep it at least half full of water all the time. No other watering will be required.

Prepare a pot or flat of rooting medium as for stem cuttings. Use sharp sand, perlite, vermiculite, or sterile potting soil to root leaf cuttings.

Select medium-size, healthy leaves for cuttings.

If the leaf has a petiole (stem), insert the cutting in the medium up to the base of the leaf. If the petiole is short or if there is no petiole, insert the cutting so that the basal portion is covered with medium. Keep rooting bed moist.

Sansevierias and rex begonias can be propagated by cuttings of only a portion of the leaf. A single leaf of sansevieria can be cut into several 2- to 4-inch

cuttings and placed in medium with the basal portion buried. Cut rex begonia along the veins of the top ⅓ of the leaf and insert the cutting in medium with the basal portion buried.

Leaf cuttings will take longer to form roots than do stem cuttings. Several weeks may elapse before leaf cuttings have formed plantlets at the base. When the plantlets are well formed, pot the rooted cuttings.

Listed below are many plants commonly propagated by leaf cuttings:

    African violet
    Rex begonia
    Echeveria
    Gloxinia
    Jade plant
    Kalanchoe (leaf plus bud)
    Peperomia
    Philodendron (leaf plus bud)
    Piggyback plant (leaf with plantlet)
    Sansevieria
    Sedum

Leaf and stem cuttings of some plants may be rooted in tap water. For the amateur gardener this is often a desirable method of propagation because it allows closer observation of the rooting process.

Propagate *Sansevieria* and other succulents from leaf cuttings.

Root entire leaves or sections of leaves.

Many plants will form roots in water. Use only 1 inch of water; the roots form near the surface of the water. Try to restrict root development to the base of the cutting.

Cuttings rooted in water must be potted when the roots are young; old roots formed in water are difficult to establish in soil. House plants easily rooted by placing cuttings in water include the following:

    African violet
    Avocado (seed)
    Begonia *(Begonia* x *semperflorens-cultorum)*
    Coleus
    Dracaena
    Fuchsia
    Gardenia
    Geranium
    Impatiens
    Ivies
    Philodendron
    Swedish ivy
    Wandering Jew

Air-layering

Many large plants with thin, leathery leaves and long main stems are propagated by a process known as air-layering. This method consists of in-

ducing new roots to grow on an upper portion of the stem without detaching that portion of the stem from the rest of the plant. Air-layering is also used to rejuvenate large plants which have dropped their bottom leaves and become unattractive as a result. New roots are formed on the stem under the healthy leaves, then the top is severed from the bottom and potted as a new plant. Such action is sometimes required with rubber plants and dieffenbachias.

Here are some plants commonly propagated by air-layering:

    Croton
    Dieffenbachia
    Fiddle-leaf fig
    Jade plant
    Monstera
    Osmanthus
    Philodendron
    Rubber plant
    Schefflera

When the lower stem of a large plant becomes bare and unsightly, it may be necessary to air-layer the plant. First, make a slanting cut about halfway into the stem several inches below the healthy section of the plant. Hold the wound open by inserting a piece of a toothpick. If you use a root-inducing hormone, apply it at this stage. Use a knife or other flat object to apply the hormone powder to surfaces of the wound. Take a handful of moist sphagnum moss. Wrap the moss around the wound. Leave the toothpick in place to keep wound surfaces exposed. Secure the moss with string. Wrap cellophane around the moss and secure it above and below the wound. After a few weeks, roots will form inside the moss ball. Remove the cellophane, cut the stem just below the new root ball, and pot the new plant.

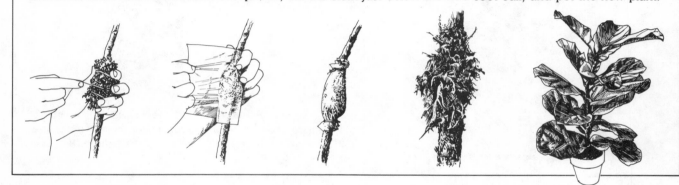

Dividing plants

Many plants grow in clumps, either with or without stems. A plant with 2 or more stems arising from the roots can usually be divided to form as many plants as there are stems. Other plants, such as sansevieria, send up thick clumps of leaves directly from the crown (top of root system). These, too, are easy to divide.

To make divisions, remove the plant from its pot and shake off as much soil as is necessary to allow you to see most of the root system. Many plants will break easily into divisions containing a healthy portion of the top with vigorous roots attached. Use a sharp knife to cut apart those divisions you cannot pull apart with your hands. Pot the new divisions immediately, before the roots dry out.

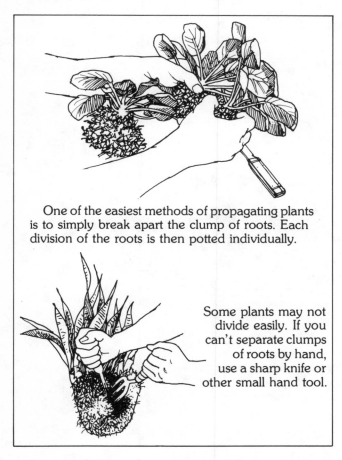

One of the easiest methods of propagating plants is to simply break apart the clump of roots. Each division of the roots is then potted individually.

Some plants may not divide easily. If you can't separate clumps of roots by hand, use a sharp knife or other small hand tool.

If some divisions have poor roots or no roots at all, insert them in peat moss and sand or peat moss and perlite until roots form. Then pot them in the appropriate potting mixture and move the plant to the recommended location.

The best time to divide plants is in the spring as new growth begins.

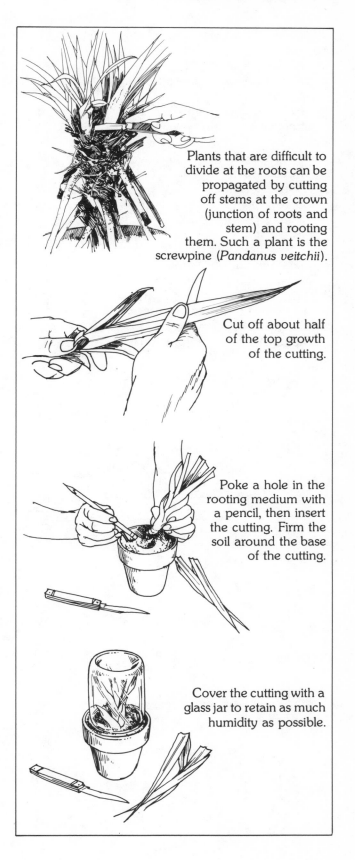

Plants that are difficult to divide at the roots can be propagated by cutting off stems at the crown (junction of roots and stem) and rooting them. Such a plant is the screwpine (*Pandanus veitchii*).

Cut off about half of the top growth of the cutting.

Poke a hole in the rooting medium with a pencil, then insert the cutting. Firm the soil around the base of the cutting.

Cover the cutting with a glass jar to retain as much humidity as possible.

The following plants are often propagated by division:

African violet
Aspidistra, Cast-iron plant
Caladium
Chinese evergreen
Echeveria
Ferns
Maranta, Prayer plant
Peperomia
Sansevieria
Screwpine
Spider plant
Succulents

Runners and suckers

The easiest plants to propagate are those that send out an elongated stem (runner) with a plantlet at the end. To propagate these, simply sever the plantlet from its stem and pot it. One of the best examples of a plant propagated in this manner is the spider plant. A thriving spider plant may have as many as 2 dozen runners with a plantlet attached to each one.

Some plants produce plantlets at the base of the mother plants. Such plantlets are called *suckers*. Use a sharp knife to cut the suckers from the mother plant, then pot the suckers in loamy potting soil. They will quickly form roots and grow to be mature plants.

Plants commonly propagated from runners and suckers include the following:

African violet
Agave
Aloe
Asparagus fern
Boston fern
Echeveria
Piggyback plant
Screwpine, Pandanus
Spider plant
Strawberry geranium, Strawberry begonia

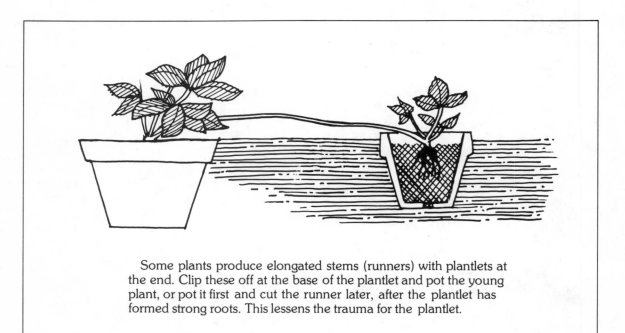

Some plants produce elongated stems (runners) with plantlets at the end. Clip these off at the base of the plantlet and pot the young plant, or pot it first and cut the runner later, after the plantlet has formed strong roots. This lessens the trauma for the plantlet.

Indoor Hanging Gardens

Perhaps the most exciting way of displaying container-grown plants is to pot them in baskets that can be hung from overhead or wall bracket supports. Hanging gardens are as old as ancient Babylon and have a special importance for today's metropolitan population whose surface space for growing plants may be limited. Hanging gardens can be single baskets or pots, or if you have very solid beams which are easy to locate, containers can be suspended one below the other to create a multi-level hanging garden.

Hanging baskets can be hung inside or outside, wherever you can provide solid support for the hangers and wherever the plant won't be in the way. Indoors, they are commonly hung in windows, in empty corners of rooms, or against walls as a refreshing alternative to mirrors, framed paintings, and posters. Plants suspended over kitchen sinks have the added benefit of increased humidity. Plants suspended above a free-standing bookcase or plant rack make interesting room dividers,

though special precautions must be taken to avoid dripping.

Locations for hanging gardens must ultimately depend on the light, temperature, and humidity requirements of the plants you wish to hang (see Chapter Two, *Caring For House Plants*). Chances are excellent, however, that there is a plant adapted to nearly any location you may choose.

An infinite variety of containers can be used as hanging baskets. Commercially available containers are usually designed from galvanized wire, plastic, terra-cotta, ceramic, or wood. In the Southwest where summer weather is hot and dry, a container

Inside or out, cascading petunias are delightful plants for hanging containers.

37

Begonia semperflorens is a spectacular hanging plant.

The most important requirement of growing plants in hanging baskets is to have the proper soil medium. It should be loamy in texture, drain well, and hold necessary moisture for the plants.

A good potting mix to use in hanging baskets is a combination of about two-thirds organic material (peat moss, compost, bark, etc.) and one-third mineral matter (soil, sand, perlite, etc.). These proportions should be adequate for proper drainage and for ample air circulation to the root system.

Once the soil is properly mixed and a small amount of slow-release fertilizer is added, the basket is ready to be planted. Purchased plants may be in pots, bands, or other containers and can be planted at any time. If they are watered before being removed from their containers, they can be taken out and separated much more easily.

Set each plant firmly in place, no deeper in the potting soil than it was previously growing. After planting, thoroughly soak the entire basket in a tub of water; then hang in position.

When summer heat is intense, the baskets must be watered at least once a day. Because hanging baskets are exposed to dry, hot air on all sides, they dry out very quickly. It is necessary to keep soil moist for good plant growth.

Watering hanging baskets and pots can be messy. One solution is to measure how much water each basket requires before excess water begins to drain through the hole in the bottom. Note also how much time elapses between waterings in this amount. Then measure that amount of water before each application. Be sure that containers have a saucer attached to catch excess water.

Feeding should be delayed until the baskets are established and growing. Because of the frequency of watering, some plant food is quickly washed away and must be replaced. Feed each week or two with a complete liquid fertilizer in mild solution. Dilute concentrated liquid solutions in water at the rate of 1½ teaspoons to a gallon of water. Apply this mild solution to hanging baskets at the rate of ½ cup per 12-inch basket.

that does not lose moisture rapidly is desirable. For this reason, solid plastic containers or wooden boxes are preferred; clay pots require twice as much watering because so much moisture evaporates through them.

It is not difficult to make an attractive hanging basket that retains moisture. Choose a wire basket and line it generously with either coarse sphagnum moss or sheet moss. Wet the moss prior to lining the basket. Plastic and papier mache liners are also available for this purpose. Next, cut a layer of polyethylene plastic to size to fit against the moss, and fill the plastic liner with potting soil mix. Then, to assure proper drainage, punch holes through the plastic in the bottom of the basket.

Select the plants to go into the basket bearing in mind the location the baskets will have—either in the sun or in the shade. Because of water requirements, hanging baskets are usually more successful when located in the shade and not exposed to hot sun. Plants of drooping habit are preferable, since their flowers and foliage are displayed to best advantage. Although trailing plants are inherently adapted for such baskets, more sedate plants can readily be used. Besides annual and perennial vines, plants such as petunia, impatiens, coleus, and lantana also lend themselves to container culture.

Supports

Don't trust nails, no matter how large they are, to hold heavy baskets or clay containers. Not only are nails undependable, but the larger the nail, the worse it looks. Hook and eye screws will hold more weight and are often available in decorative designs. If you buy an eye screw and your hanger also has a

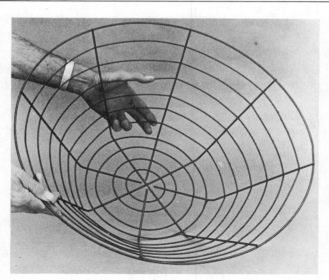

A. Select a galvanized wire basket.

B. Line the basket with moist sheet moss, green side out. Next, cut a circular piece of polyethylene plastic with which to line the inside of the basket.

C. Fill the basket with a soil mixture of 3 parts organic matter (peat moss, leaf mold, finely ground compost) to 1 part loam and 1 part sand or perlite.

D. Plant rooted cuttings around the outside edge of the basket so that they will cascade over the sides.

E. Plant the center of the basket with upright, dwarfish plants. A good combination is variegated wanderingjew around the rim and common coleus in the center.

loop at the end, you'll need to purchase an S hook (shaped like the letter S) to connect them.

Most ceilings are made of gypsum board or plaster over lath. Hook and *eye* screws will easily be pulled out of these by the weight of the basket. Locate a beam in the ceiling (*beams*, also called *joists*, are heavy boards, usually 2 × 6s or 2 × 8s, against which the ceiling is mounted) by tapping with your knuckles along the ceiling until the sound becomes less hollow and you feel something solid behind the gypsum board or plaster. Beams are spaced as close as 16 inches apart or as far as 24 inches apart and farther. Determine the direction one beam runs in order to determine the pattern of all the support beams; then notice how the location of beams affects your choice of locations for the basket.

Once you have settled on a place to hang the basket (taking into account light exposure, dripping, humidity, and exposure to drafts as well as location of beams), drill a pilot hole and screw in the eye or hook until you can no longer see the threads in the screw.

False ceilings usually have no wooden joists. If this is the case in your home, use wall brackets. Baskets which are half-round are available for wall hangers; single hanging containers may be mounted on them. Or purchase racks in which to set two or more small pots.

Walls, like ceilings, are made of soft materials that will not support the weight of a potted plant. The outer materials are mounted on a series of vertical beamlike structures called *studs*. Tap on the wall with your knuckles until you locate a stud. Wall studs are usually spaced about 16 inches apart. When you locate a wall stud that is in a convenient place to hang plants, drill a pilot hole and screw in the wall mounts and brackets.

Hangers

Most hanging containers are sold with hangers, but you may wish to hang some other container you have. You can buy hangers at the garden supply store, or you can make them yourself.

Hangers either attach to the rim of the container or they loop under it and cradle it. The variety of hangers is nearly as vast as that of the containers at your disposal. Wire, chain, rope, plastic, macramé, leather, and braided fabric are all materials that can be used to make hangers. Rim hangers are best made from wire, chain, and plastic. Cradle hangers are made from the more supple materials such as rope, leather, macrame, and braided fabric.

Be certain that whatever material you choose or whatever type of hanger you buy, it will support the plant and the container you have in mind.

How To Hang a Basket

Tap the ceiling with the handle of a hammer until you locate a beam. Once you've located a beam, drill into it.

Insert a hook screw and use a screwdriver to help twist it into the hole. Attach a swivel hook to the hook screw. The swivel hook will allow the basket to turn freely.

FOLIAGE PLANTS FOR HANGING BASKETS

Common name	Latin name	Light requirements
Asparagus fern	*Asparagus sp.*	sun/light shade in South
Baby's-tears	*Soleirolia soleirolii*	sun/light shade
Bear's-foot fern	*Humata tyermannii*	shade
Boston fern	*Nephrolepis exaltata* Bostoniensis	shade
Bridal veil, Wandering Jew	*Gibasis geniculata*	light shade
Coleus	*Coleus blumei*	sun indoors, shade outdoors
Donkey's-tail	*Sedum morganianum*	sun or shade
English ivy	*Hedera helix*	shade
Grape ivy	*Cissus rhombifolia*	sun or shade
Peperomia	*Peperomia sp.*	light shade
Philodendron	*Philodendron cordatum*	light shade
Piggyback plant, Pick-a-back-plant	*Tolmiea menziesii*	sun/light shade
Prayer plant	*Maranta leuconeura*	light shade
Rosary vine	*Ceropegia woodii*	sun indoors/shade outdoors
Spider plant	*Chlorophytum comosum*	light shade
Swedish ivy	*Plectranthus australis*	shade
Wandering Jew	*Tradescantia fluminensis* *Zebrina pendula*	sun indoors/light shade outdoors

FLOWERING PLANTS FOR HANGING BASKETS

Common name	Latin name	Light requirements	Flower color
Begonia	*Begonia* x *semperflorens-cultorum*	light shade	red, pink, rose, salmon, orange yellow, white
Black-eyed Susan vine	*Thunbergia alata*	sun	orange, yellow, white
Bougainvillea	*Bougainvillea sp.*	sun/light shade in South	red
Browallia	*Browallia speciosa*	sun/light shade	blue, purple
Christmas cactus	*Schlumbergera bridgesii*	sun/light shade in South	red
Fuchsia	*Fuchsia* x *hybrida*	sun/light shade in South	red, pink, purple, blue, white, bicolors
Geranium	*Pelargonium sp.*	sun/light shade	red, pink, purple, lavender, white
Impatiens	*Impatiens sp.*	light shade	red, pink, orange, violet, white, bicolors
Italian bellflower	*Campanula isophylla*	sun/light shade	pale blue, white
Kalanchoe	*Kalanchoe blossfeldiana*	sun	red
Lantana, trailing	*Lantana montevidensis*	sun	pink, purple, yellow, cream
Morning glory	*Ipomoea sp.*	sun	red, blue, white
Shrimp plant	*Beloperone guttata*	light shade	white spotted purple
Snow-in-summer	*Cerastium tomentosum*	sun/shade in South	white
Sweet alyssum	*Lobularia maritima*	sun/light shade	pink, purple, white
Wax plant	*Hoya carnosa*	sun	white

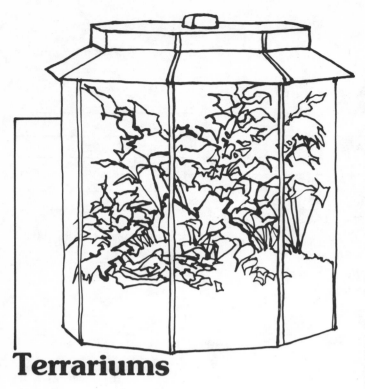

Terrariums

Terrariums, miniature gardens in closed glass containers, are more popular today than ever before. Anyone can be successful with terrarium culture; it is an essentially carefree way to grow plants. Since terrariums do well under artificial light and are not affected by low humidity, they are particularly appealing to apartment dwellers with no outdoor gardening space.

Constructing the terrarium

There are many containers that can serve as a terrarium: brandy snifters, apothecary jars, aquariums, fish bowls, and bottles of all shapes and sizes. The container size is limited only by the number and scale of plants you wish to put into it. A glass container is usually preferable to plastic because it does not scratch or discolor as easily. If a cover is not provided, one can be improvised with a piece of glass or plastic that seals tightly.

Once the container is chosen, clean it with soap and water, and dry it until it is spotless. In the bottom of the container, place a layer of clean gravel topped with a small amount of charcoal granules to aid in keeping the soil from becoming too acid. Add sterilized soil mix, available at garden supply stores, to the desired level. If the opening of the container is small, use a funnel to get the soil in without getting the sides dirty. To avoid splattering plants with soil, add all the soil you intend to use before you begin to set the plants. Be sure the soil is moist, but not wet, before it is put into the container. Next, set the

plants in place, using long-handled spoons, forks, or sticks as necessary.

After planting, water just enough to settle the plants. Leave the terrarium uncovered for a day or two to see if the plants are going to survive, then cover the opening of the container to maintain humidity inside. Place the terrarium where it will receive plenty of light but no direct sunlight.

Terrariums need very little additional moisture; add only a small amount of water if plants show slight wilting.

Fertilizer, if used at all, should be applied very sparingly lest the plants outgrow their container too quickly.

There are many plants available for use in terrariums. Choose them wisely. It is particularly important to group plants that require a similar environment. Select dwarf varieties and low-growing plants so you can enjoy them for a longer period of time.

Either native or tropical plants may be selected for terrariums. Most small plants that grow in a damp, tree-covered forest area will do well in the moist atmosphere of a terrarium. Small house plants, such

A Simple Terrarium

A. Place washed gravel and charcoal granules in the bottom of the terrarium and add 1 inch of soil.

B. Set plants in position, cover roots with soil, and gently firm the soil around the roots.

D. Use pebbles and stone chips around the plants as a decorative ground cover.

C. Mist the plants lightly to wash dust from the foliage and moisten the soil.

E. Cover the terrarium after it is completed. Water should not be necessary for several months.

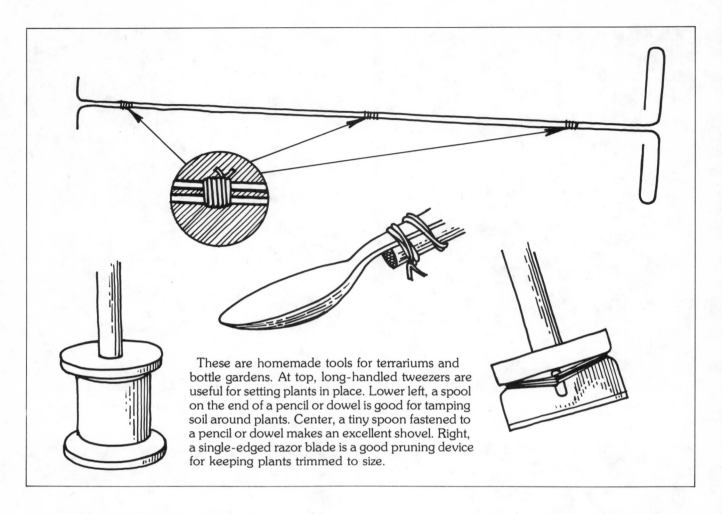

These are homemade tools for terrariums and bottle gardens. At top, long-handled tweezers are useful for setting plants in place. Lower left, a spool on the end of a pencil or dowel is good for tamping soil around plants. Center, a tiny spoon fastened to a pencil or dowel makes an excellent shovel. Right, a single-edged razor blade is a good pruning device for keeping plants trimmed to size.

as miniature African violets, tropical ferns, ivy, and peperomia, may be combined for an easy-to-care-for terrarium. Forest mosses are also excellent.

Types of terrariums

The type of terrarium you build is determined by your selection of plants. Because a terrarium is a closed mini-environment, providing a uniform climate throughout, plants requiring similar growing conditions must be chosen. It is useful in building a terrarium to consider plants in two cultural groupings, woodland terrariums and tropical terrariums.

Woodland terrariums. The best plants for woodland terrariums can probably be found within a few miles of your home. Cover the floor of the terrarium with mosses and lichens. Not only will these lend a forest floor effect, but the bits of sod will also provide anchorage for plant roots.

You can buy plants for a terrarium or, for a woodland terrarium, you can dig them yourself if you first obtain permission from the owner of the property where you wish to dig. Select only small, fine-textured plants for a terrarium and be sure to collect a portion of the root system with soil still attached to the roots. Place plants in a plastic sandwich bag to transport them home. Transplant them into the terrarium as soon as possible to assure their survival. After a day or two, cover the opening of the terrarium to maintain the level of moisture and humidity inside the container.

Tropical terrariums. Construction of a tropical terrarium is much like that of a woodland terrarium except in the selection of plants. Since most common house plants are native to the tropics, selecting plant material is not difficult; rooted cuttings or offsets of plants such as spider plant or babystears are good to begin with. Small plants with finely textured foliage are best suited to the tiny world of the terrarium.

An excellent way to create a miniature desert scene is in a dish garden. Use a shallow dish or clay saucer with equal parts sand and peat moss. Cover the soil mix with a light layer of sand to give the entire dish garden a uniform appearance. Such a minature garden is not enclosed.

Troubles in miniature worlds

If moisture accumulates on the walls of your terrarium and runs down the sides, there is too much moisture inside. Remove the top and ventilate the terrarium for 15 to 30 minutes. Spots of mold on plants or decor in the terrarium may indicate inadequate light as well as excessive moisture. Remove rotting leaves or plants, ventilate for 15 to 30 minutes, then relocate the terrarium in a brighter place. Avoid direct sunlight however.

Wilting of plants is due to inadequate moisture. Water the terrarium by misting. Mist the plants and soil very lightly (3 or 4 squirts of the spray bottle) every hour until wilting is checked and plants look

Top row: Peperomia obtusifolia, minature fern, Syngonium sp. Center row: Golden baby's-tears (Soleirolia sp.), baby's-tears (S. soleirolii), silver tree (Pilea sp.). Bottom row: Minature fern, spreading clubmoss (Selaginella sp.), strawberry geranium (Saxifraga stolonifera).

healthy again. If the terrarium tends to dry out rapidly, it may be receiving too much light and heat.

Plants that outgrow their space in the terrarium must be removed and potted separately. Fill the empty areas with plants in better proportion to the rest of the terrarium.

Prune back fast growing plants from time to time, especially if they begin to crowd other plants. This will considerably extend the life of the terrarium.

Terrariums are not immortal; eventually all the plants will outgrow the container and will need to be replaced. At this point, it may be a good idea to empty the container and start afresh with a clean container and fresh, sterilized soil.

Top row: Sanders dracaena *(D. sanderiana),* minature palm *(Chamaedorea erumpens),* podocarpus *(P. macrophyllus* Maki). *Center row:* False aralia *(Dizygotheca elegantissima),* a dwarf Warneckii dracaena *(D. deremensis* Warneckii),* variegated Swedish ivy *(Plectranthus australis* Variegata). *Bottom row:* Emerald Ripple peperomia, panamiga *(Pilea involucrata),* aluminum plant *(Pilea cadierei).*

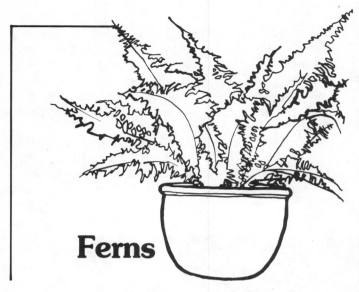

Ferns

Ferns are perhaps the most popular indoor-outdoor plants in the United States. Their exacting culture is simplified if only we keep in mind their usual habitat—the shady, moist woods. As indoor plants, ferns are incomparable for their ability to bring the feeling of the forest indoors. No plant imports a mass of greenery into the home faster than a large fern. From the delicate, airy fronds of the maidenhair fern (*Adiantum cuneatum*) to the massive Goldie's fern (*Dryopteris goldiana*) with fronds 4 to 5 feet long and 1½ feet wide, ferns can be used decoratively in floor planters, pots, or hanging baskets. Ferns are also used in bouquets and arrangements of cut flowers. One caution: ferns are not considered easy plants to grow. Beginners might start with Boston fern.

A wide variety of ferns is available from garden stores and greenhouses, or you may transplant them yourself from the woods although few native species are satisfactory house plants. It is important to provide the correct soil and growing conditions for indoor ferns. Soil must be rich in organic matter and kept evenly moist. Cool temperatures, medium to high humidity, and filtered shade are all necessary for success with ferns. Once the correct conditions are provided, ferns are among the least demanding of all indoor plants.

Locate ferns in a north window in a bathroom or in a hallway or room where there is no direct sunlight. Bathrooms are recommended because the

Left to right: Occidental fern *(Polypodium sp.)*, Fluffy-ruffle fern *(Nephrolepis exaltata* Fluffy-ruffles), New Zealand cliffbrake fern *(Pellaea rotundifolia)*, bear's-paw fern *(Aglaomorpha meyeniana)*.

atmosphere is usually cooler and more humid than in other rooms.

Mix garden loam with leaf mold, compost, peat moss, or ground fir bark to obtain the peaty soil required for ferns. Like all soil for indoor plants, soil for ferns should be sterilized in the oven. For sterilizing instructions *see* Chapter Two, *Soil for House Plants*.

Provide a container with good drainage. Most ferns require an evenly moist soil, but be careful not to overwater. The soil should never be soggy.

Fertilizer requirements are minimal for ferns that are potted in compost. Apply fertilizer every 3 months during the growing season, but withhold fertilizer from November to February. Fish emulsion is a good fertilizer for ferns, but any other commonly available house plant food will also be sufficient.

Repot ferns annually in the spring and divide crowns to obtain several plants. If crowns (top of the root system from which stems grow) do not easily pull apart by hand, cut them into sections with a sharp knife. Pot each section of crown individually.

Propagation of most ferns is done by dividing crowns at repotting time. Ferns are also propagated

Asparagus fern (upper left) and two Boston ferns

Staghorn ferns (*Platycerium bifurcatum*)

from spores (seeds). Growing ferns from spores is an exacting practice and not completely practical unless you have greenhouse facilities. For the adventurous indoor gardener, however, here is how it is done: watch the undersides of fronds carefully to know when spore cases begin to split open. This indicates that spores are ripe. Remove the frond and place it on a sheet of white paper with the underside down. In a day or two, the spore cases will have emptied the spores onto the paper. Sow spores in a pot or flat with about 3 inches of sterilized soil which has been finely sifted. Sprinkle spores on the soil and set the pot in water to subirrigate the soil until it is wet nearly to the top. Set the pot in 2 inches of wet vermiculite or sphagnum moss and cover the pot with cellophane or a large inverted jar. If mold forms on the soil surface, remove the cellophane covering for a day or two to allow the surface to dry out. If excessive surface moisture is not a problem, mist the surface gently every other day. Place the pot in filtered sunlight or under fluorescent lights to germinate the spores. Germination should take place in 4 to 21 days, depending on the species. In 1 to 3 months, growth will be visible without the use of a magnifying glass. Do not overwater. Excessive watering promotes the growth of fungus diseases, especially the disease called damping-off which

causes the sudden rotting of seedling plants at the soil level.

In about two years, the young ferns will be large enough to pot.

Insects and diseases are rarely a problem on mature ferns. Be on the lookout for scale insects (*see* Chapter Four, *Curing Plant Ailments*). If infestation is light, pick the insects off by hand. Serious infestation will require the use of an insecticide.

Ferns for indoors

A number of ferns are popular indoor plants. The following are some of the more commonly grown species:

Name	Size
Bear's-foot fern (*Humata tyermannii*)	small
Bear's-paw fern (*Aglaomorpha meyeniana*)	medium to large
Bird's-nest fern (*Asplenium nidus*)	medium
Boston fern, Sword fern (*Nephrolepis exaltata* Bostoniensis)	small to large
Fluffy ruffles (*Nephrolepis exaltata* Fluffy Ruffles)	medium to large
Golden polypody (*Polypodium aureum*)	medium
Japanese holly fern (*Cyrtomium falcatum*)	small to medium
Maidenhair fern (*Adiantum cunecitum*)	medium
Occidental fern (*Polypodium occidentale*)	medium to very large
Rabbit's-foot fern, (*Polypodium aureum*)	small to medium
Staghorn fern (*Platycerium bifurcatum*)	small to large
Cretan brake fern (*Pteris cretica*)	small to medium

Bulbs

Fragrance gardening is easier with bulbs than with any other group of flowering plants. The selection of fragrant bulbs is wide and can provide a succession of delightful scents throughout the year.

No flowering plants respond to indoor culture better than bulbs. Some bulbs, such as amaryllis or canna, may be kept in containers for years at a time, requiring no more attention than the simplest house plants. They may be potted at any time of year and forced into bloom after 4 to 6 weeks of proper storage. Store the bulbs in the vegetable crisper of the refrigerator to provide a temperature of about 40 degrees. Many bulbs must have this rest period in a cool location in order to flower satisfactorily.

You may buy bulbs already potted and ready to grow or you can pot them yourself.

Containers include clay and plastic pots or, if you have none of these, shallow bowls.

Amaryllis (*Hippeastrum* sp.)

Media used in container bulb culture are coarse peat moss, pebbles and water, or soil mix.

Bulb fiber is a mixture of coarse peat, sand (or crushed shell), and powdered charcoal. Soak the fiber and squeeze it out. Fill a bowl or shallow pot almost to the top and, pressing the fiber down, leave a slight depression in the center. Place the first bulb in the center, and position the others around it so the bulbs support each other.

How To Plant Bulbs in a Container

After cleaning the container, fill the pot one-third full with gravel or plastic foam packing "peanuts."

Cover foam with soil mix; then crowd bulbs together in the pot so that they support each other.

Fill the container with additional soil mix, leaving only the neck of the bulbs exposed. Water thoroughly.

50

A mix of equal parts potting soil, perlite or vermiculite, and peat moss is a good rooting medium. Fill the pot nearly full, soak, and allow the water to drain. Form a slight depression in the center and place a bulb in it. Place bulbs around the central bulb so each supports the other.

Pebbles and water are the simplest media for forcing bulbs. Select a bowl or dish at least 3 inches deep and fill the bottom with a 1-inch layer of charcoal. Add to this about 1½ inches of clean ¾-inch pebbles. Add enough water to reach the bottoms of the bulbs. If you use a pot, plug the drainage hole in the bottom with a cork.

Always purchase first quality bulbs for forcing. Stored within the bulbs are all the ingredients necessary for the successful growth of roots, foliage, and flowers. If inferior bulbs are purchased, results are usually disappointing.

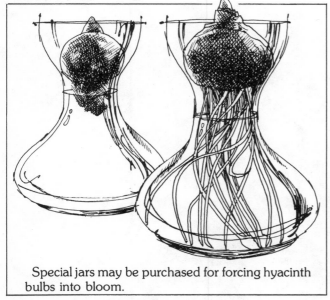

Special jars may be purchased for forcing hyacinth bulbs into bloom.

Don't be afraid to crowd bulbs in container planting. With large bulbs, such as narcissus and tulips, place at least 5 bulbs in an 8-inch pot or 6 to 8 bulbs in a 10-inch pot. With very large bulbs, such as hyacinths, place 1 bulb in a 4-inch pot, 3 bulbs in an 8-inch pot, or 5 to 6 bulbs in a 10-inch pot.

Before planting, place 1 inch of gravel or potsherds in the bottom of the container. Then fill the pot with soil mix and place the bulbs as directed above. Cover the bulbs with soil mix so that the tips are just beneath the surface. Leave the tips of tulips, hyacinths, and daffodils exposed.

When planting in bowls or other shallow containers, fill the bottom with pebbles. Over this, add an equal volume of vermiculite, soil mixture, or bulb fiber. Place bulbs in the container and fill in around them with more vermiculite or bulb fiber. Fill the bottom of the container with water to the bottoms of the bulbs.

Keep the planted bulbs in a cold, dark place for about 3 months. Then place the pots in a cool, bright location until foliage develops. New leaves will be light green, but will darken as they mature. When this happens, move the pots to a sunny window. Once flowering begins, keep the pots out of the direct sun or extreme heat. It may be necessary to water the plants occasionally since the low humidity indoors will cause them to dry out quickly.

Bulbs that have been forced rarely bloom the next year. However, many bulbs may be planted in the garden, where they can rebuild energy to bloom again. When the flowers fade, remove them so they won't go to seed. Continue watering the foliage and make a light application of liquid plant food. When the foliage begins to fade, remove the bulbs from the pots and store in a dark, cool, dry location until fall. Plant in the garden at that time.

Callas are easy to grow indoors.

Tulips seldom bloom satisfactorily a second time. After forcing tulips, discard the old bulbs and start new ones.

Here are the bulbs most favored for indoor culture:

Achimenes	Galanthus
Agapanthus	Gladiolus
Amaryllis	Hyacinth
Begonia (tuberous)	Iris (some species)
Caladium	Lily
Calla	Narcissus
Canna	Oxalis
Crinum	Spiderlily
Crocus	Sternbergia
Cyclamen	Tuberose
Freesia	Tulip

Hyacinth selections which respond to forcing include Amethystinus and City of Haarlem. Popular daffodil selections include Paperwhite Grandiflora, Fortune, King Alfred, Yellow Cheerfulness, Thalia, Unsurpassable, Mount Hood, and Peeping Tom. Tulip selections include General Eisenhower, Mrs. John T. Scheepers, Insurpassable, Queen of Bartigon, Orange Favorite, Queen of Sheba, White Triumphator, Gudoshnik, and Garden Party.

Some bulbs can be forced indoors only once; then they must be planted outside if another bloom season is expected. These include crocus, freesia, galanthus, gladiolus, hyacinth, lily, narcissus (including daffodils), spiderlily, and sternbergia.

Cyclamen

Cacti and Succulents

Cacti and succulents are among the most unusual house plants. Because of their ability to grow in hot, dry conditions such as the desert, cacti and succulents make ideal house plants. Granted the average home is not desertlike, but the amount of moisture in the air is quite low. For this reason, many tropical or forest plants will not adapt to conditions inside the home, whereas cacti and other succulents may find indoor conditions ideal.

Any plant with thick, fleshy leaves or stems that is capable of storing large quantities of water in those fleshy parts is called a succulent. Although succulents do not constitute a family in themselves, over 8,000 species of plants are included in this grouping. Some well-known succulents are jade plant, echeveria, sedum, and crown-of-thorns. Also included in the succulent group are over 2,000 species of cactus.

Cacti are leafless plants with thick, fleshy stems that are usually covered with prickly spines. The thick stems are capable of storing large quantities of moisture to see the plant through weeks on end of rainless desert weather. Most cacti have shallow roots which allow the immediate absorbtion of the scant rain it is accustomed to receiving. Although, to many, the fantastic forms in which cacti grow are disturbing and bizarre, the fascination of these dramatic plants grows as you become more familiar with them.

The variety of plant sizes and forms to be found

A cactus planter adds drama to the indoor landscape.

Aloe, also called Burn plant

among succulents is vast indeed. It is not difficult to find succulents that lend themselves to every type of display situation from miniature gardens for the coffee table, to hanging specimens, or large upright cacti for rooms with high ceilings.

Succulents and cacti are among the easiest house plants to care for. They require less watering than most plants, adapt easily to the humidity and temperature found in homes, and usually require less frequent repotting due to their slow rate of growth.

Give a cactus the sunniest location in your home. Other succulents also need a bright location but do not overexpose them to direct sunlight as the leaves may get scorched. A major difference, in fact, between cactus and other succulents is that the latter have not lost their leaves in the course of evolution. Most plants with leaves are more susceptible to scorch damage than plants without. If you use artificial light, provide at least 800 foot-candles for cacti and at least 500 foot-candles for succulents (see Chapter Two, *Using Artificial Lighting*).

Soil for cacti and other succulents should be sandy. Mix 2 parts sand or perlite with 1 part loam and 1 part peat moss. As for other house plants, soil for succulents and cacti should be sterilized (see Chapter Two, *Soil For House Plants*). A little charcoal in the soil increases the water-absorbtion capacity of the soil mixture.

The dangers of overwatering succulents are great. Cacti have developed in areas where rainfall is constantly sparse and, as an evolutionary consequence, do not have the type of feeder roots that can take up a great quantity of moisture at one time. Other succulents, by contrast, have developed in climates that are subject to heavy rainfall followed by long periods of drought. Depending on the size of the plant and the type of container used, most succulents will need watering every 5 to 7 days during the growing season (February to November) if the pot is clay or other porous material. Those in plastic or ceramic containers will require even less watering.

Echeveria gigantea, also called Painted lady, Plush plant, or Mexican snowball.

A dish garden of succulents

Allow soil to dry partially between waterings, but not to the point where the plants shrivel.

During the dormant season (November to February) water cactus every 7 to 10 days or just enough to keep it from shriveling. Water only on dry, sunny days when the plant's roots and moisture-absorbing tissues are most receptive. Use lukewarm water or water that has been allowed to sit for an hour or two at room temperature. Cold water can injure some succulents.

Average home temperatures are suitable for succulents. If, however, you expect your cactus to bloom, it needs cool temperatures during the winter; about 45° at night and 50° to 65° during the day. A sunny, enclosed porch where the temperature does not drop below 45° is an ideal place to winter your cactus. A sunny basement window may also be a good location.

Fertilize cacti and succulents every three or four months during the growing season. (Christmas cactus needs fertilizer monthly except in winter.) Use any house plant fertilizer according to label directions.

Repot succulents, including cacti, at least once every 2 years. The best time to repot them is in the spring as new growth begins, but if your plants become too crowded, don't wait until spring to repot them. To avoid pricking yourself on cactus spines, fold a single sheet of newspaper into a strap with which to grasp the stalk and remove the plant from its container. Select a container at least 2 inches larger in diameter than the old one. If the plant is globular the pot should be 1 inch greater in diameter than the plant. Good drainage is crucial for cacti and succulents, so be sure to provide a 1-inch layer of pebbles or charcoal in the bottom of the new container. Repot succulents other than cacti in the same way you would other house plants (see Chapter Two, *Repotting House Plants*).

Old man cactus (*Cephalocereus senilis*)

Propagate cacti and succulents from divisions, stem and leaf cuttings, and seeds. Many of these plants produce offsets (young plants) around the base of the mother plant and these need only be removed from the mother plant (include a portion of the root system) and potted. If the plantlets do not separate easily in your hands, use a sharp knife to make the divisions.

Leaf cuttings may be rooted in sand or perlite mixed equally with soil. Make cuttings of a whole leaf or part of a leaf. Allow the cut end to dry out for 2 or 3 days before inserting it in the rooting medium. Crassula, gasteria, haworthia, and kalan-

choe are all easily propagated by this method. The best time to take cuttings is spring, when new growth is beginning.

Succulents and cacti can also be grown from seed planted in pots or seed flats (see Chapter five, *Propagating House Plants*).

Grafting is another popular technique for propagating cactus. Globular cacti or clusters of small, rounded cacti can be grafted onto flat, upright stems of opuntia, euphorbia, or cereus cactus. This is sometimes the only way to root difficult species. This method of culture also promotes vigorous, sometimes spectacular, growth.

Grafting Cactus

A grafted cactus is composed of a root and stem (understock) and top (scion). Cathedral cactus (left) is one of the commonly used understocks. Nearly any appropriately sized scion can be grafted successfully to a sturdy understock.

After removing the roots from the scion (top), make another thin slice with a sharp knife at the bottom of the scion.

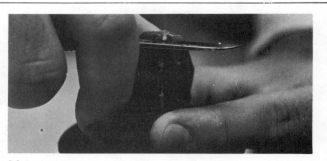

Make a thin slice on the top of the understock where the scion will come in contact.

Using a paper towel to handle the prickly scion, press the freshly cut surface of the scion against the fresh cut in the understock. For the graft to be successful, the diameter of the slice in the scion should match the diameter of the slice at the bottom of the scion.

Secure the scion on the understock with rubber bands until the graft union has formed.

Bromeliads

Some plants need no soil around their roots and can absorb moisture and nutrients directly from the air through their leaves. Such plants are called *epiphytes*. The roots of epiphytes cling to trees, stones, or other supports that will allow them to "breathe."

The nearly 20 genera of bromeliads include both epiphytic and terrestrial types. Many species bloom only once in their lives and then die, but the blooms are so dramatic and haunting that they are well worth the wait. Foliage of bromeliads is extraordinarily varied. Many have leaves arranged in cuplike rosettes that aid the plants in obtaining moisture from the atmosphere. Among the best genera for indoor growing are *Aechmea, Cryptanthus, Guzmania, Neoregelia, Tillandsia,* and *Vriesea.*

Most bromeliads like brightly lighted rooms, especially windows that are not in direct sun. If you summer your plants outdoors (a practice especially recommended for bromeliads), place them in open shade, such as that found under a tree. In fact, they are quite handsomely displayed hanging from trees as they do in their natural habitat. The even regularity and long "day" provided by artificial lighting are ideal for bromeliads. Provide at least 500 footcandles for satisfactory results (see Chapter Two, *Using Artificial Lighting*).

Bromeliads thrive in a humid environment. Mist plants every day or use an electric humidifier. A humidifier accomplishes the dual purpose of providing moisture in the air as well as circulating it. Good circulation and ventilation as well as humidity are essential to success with bromeliads. Lacking a humidifier, you can raise the humidity around a plant by placing potted bromeliads on a shallow tray of pebbles filled nearly to the top with water.

Daytime temperatures for bromeliads should be between 65° and 75°. The ideal nighttime temperature range is 55° to 65°. However, the plants are not damaged by near freezing nights or by hot summer days. Indoors, keep them out of drafts.

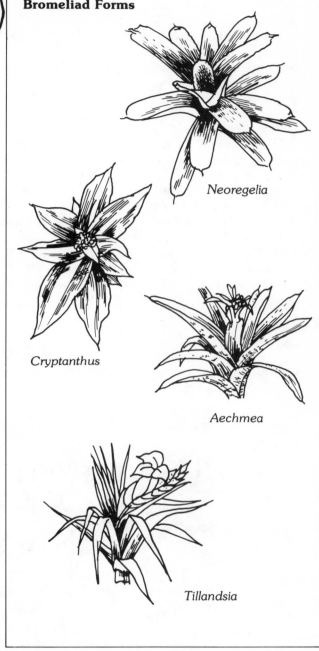

Bromeliad Forms

Neoregelia

Cryptanthus

Aechmea

Tillandsia

Watering bromeliads is easy; keep the cuplike leaf rosettes filled with water. Water the roots only occasionally and then avoid overwatering.

Fertilize bromeliads monthly from February to early November, but withhold fertilizer during the winter. Using a very mild liquid solution (see Chapter Two, *Fertilizing House Plants*), apply fertilizer to the rosettes as you would water.

Few insects attack bromeliads. It never hurts, though, to be on the lookout for scales and mealybugs. If you should detect either of these, pick them off by hand or wash them off with soapy water and an old toothbrush. If the infestation becomes rampant before you discover it, spray the plants with malathion or rotenone.

Propagation of bromeliads is simple. Each plant produces offsets or baby plants that grow at the base of the mother plant. These can be left attached to the mother plant for a display that will become increasingly spectacular as the offsets mature and bloom, or you can detach them and display them separately when the offsets are about ⅓ the size of the parent plants. With a sharp knife, remove the offset as near as possible to the mother plant. Trim excess growth from the cut end and remove withered leaves. Pot the offset in a sandy potting mix, or wrap the basal portion of the offset in moist sphagnum moss and display it on a wall or on a bromeliad tree.

Bromeliad tree

A bromeliad "tree" is an unusual and arresting way to display bromeliads. Because they absorb moisture and nutrients through the leaves rather than the roots, epiphytic bromeliads do not require that their roots be submerged in soil, water, or other root-supporting medium. Therefore, they can be attached with wire to fences, walls, rocks, and other aboveground supports.

To make a bromeliad tree, you'll need an attractive piece of driftwood, preferably with wide splits or other pockets in which to put the plants. You'll also need plastic-coated wire or nylon hose, wirecutters, sphagnum moss, and your favorite bromeliads.

First, wrap the plant's roots with sphagnum moss. If natural openings are present in the wood, place the roots in the openings and pack with additional moss to secure the plants.

The plants can also be attached directly to limbs of the driftwood with plastic-coated wire or strips of nylon hose. Be sure to use plastic-coated wire because regular or uncoated wire has a tendency to promote decay at the point of contact with the plant.

If the driftwood is large and needs support to make it stand upright, place it in a container and cement in place with plaster of Paris.

Once the tree is finished, maintenance is simple. Keep the cups formed by the leaves filled with water. Add a mild solution of liquid fertilizer once a month.

Bromeliads, because their roots do not need soil, can be tied to fences, walls, or driftwood. This bromeliad "tree" is easy to make.

A Bromeliad Tree

A. To make a bromeliad tree, first wrap roots in sphagnum moss, then lodge roots in the cracks in a piece of driftwood.

B. Secure the plants to the driftwood with plastic-coated wire or with strips of nylon hose.

Favorite Foliage Plants

Aluminum plant

Among the easiest plants to grow are the aluminum plant *(Pilea cadierei)* and the artillery plant *(P. microphylla)*. Both are small- to medium-size plants and are well displayed on sills, end tables, and other tight places where most plants might look crowded. Standard aluminum plants grow no taller than 10 or 12 inches and the dwarf forms grow 5 to 6 inches tall. The leaves are elliptic and puffy with depressed veins. The artillery plant has small, fernlike leaves arranged along both sides of the branches. Because of its fine texture, the artillery plant is a popular specimen for terrariums and miniature gardens. Both plants are native to the New World tropics.

Locate *Pilea* in a sunny south window or in a bright room. Its small size makes it ideal for window sills and tables. If artificial light is used, provide at least 400 footcandles.

Keep soil slightly moist at all times. This means light, frequent waterings. Provide a temperature range of 60° to 75° and low humidity.

Wait 3 or 4 months before feeding new plants. Fertilize established plants monthly with a weak liquid fertilizer solution.

Repot *Pilea* each year, using 3- or 4-inch pots. Artillery plants grow best in loamy soil with liberal amounts of peat moss or fine compost. A mix of 2 parts peat moss, 1 part garden loam, and 1 part sand (or perlite) is sufficient.

In early spring, pinch back stems to promote branching and encourage bushier plants. These clippings can be rooted to grow new plants. *Pilea* is also propagated from seeds and by dividing the roots of overcrowded plants. When artillery plants become leggy and unkempt, discard them and start new plants from cuttings of the old.

Left: artillery plant *(Pilea microphylla)*. *Right:* aluminum plant *(P. cadierei)*.

Asparagus fern *(Asparagus setaceus)*

Asparagus fern

The light, airy texture of asparagus fern *(Asparagus setaceus* or *Asparagus sprengeri)* contrasts pleasingly with the foliage of most other house plants. The tall stalks may be displayed upright, or they may be trained to sprawl and arch over the sides of hanging containers. The foliage is an attractive touch in cut flower arrangements or in a tall vase by itself. Foxtail asparagus fern *(Asparagus meyerii)* produces upright stalks of dense, furry foliage. All asparagus ferns are easy to grow and recommended for the beginner.

Locate asparagus fern in medium to bright light, but avoid direct sunlight as it may damage the delicate foliage. When using artificial lighting, provide 400 to 500 footcandles.

Soil for asparagus ferns should be loamy and kept slightly moist all the time. Recommended temperatures for asparagus fern are 50° to 65° at night and 65° to 75° during the day. Medium humidity is sufficient for good growth.

Fertilize established plants monthly, but do not fertilize newly potted or repotted plants for at least 2 months. Be careful to spill no fertilizer on the delicate leaves of asparagus fern. Repot overcrowded plants at any time of the year.

Propagate asparagus fern at any time by dividing clumps of roots. Cut old stalks off at soil level. New stalks will soon arise. Asparagus fern can also be grown from seeds.

Baby's-tears

Because of the fine texture of the stems and leaves, baby's-tears *(Soleirolia soleirolii)* have long been favorite subjects for terrariums and bottle gardens. They are also ideal for narrow shelves and window sills with a northern exposure.

Baby's-tears is a small plant with many trailing stems and tiny rounded leaves. Flowers are minute and of no ornamental value. Native to the Mediterranean islands of Sardinia and Corsica, these weedy little plants are often found growing on greenhouse floors where parts of plants have fallen unnoticed and taken root.

Locate baby's-tears in medium light. When using artificial light, provide at least 400 footcandles.

Soil should be loamy and kept moist. Baby's-tears grow best in cool, humid conditions. Night temperatures should be 55° to 60°; day temperatures 60° to 70°.

Fertilize established plants monthly. Do not fertilize newly potted or repotted plants for at least 2 months. Repotting may be done at any time of the year.

Propagation of baby's-tears is easy and can be done at any time of the year. Root stem cuttings in water, or propagate by dividing clumps of overcrowded plants when repotting.

Baby's-tears *(Soleirolia soleirolii)*

Rex begonia

Of the many types of begonias available, the one grown for its striking and colorful foliage is *Begonia* x *rex-cultorum*. Leaves are large, thick, and red, burgundy, pink, silver, or lavender. A number of bicolored types are also available. Though most types of rex begonia produce small pink flowers, these are not nearly as spectacular as the foliage.

Locate begonias in medium light or indirect sunlight during most of the year, but during late fall and winter, rex begonias should receive 3 or 4 hours of direct sunlight each day. When using artificial light, provide up to 800 footcandles during late fall and winter and 500 during the rest of the year.

Grow rex begonia in peaty soil. Keep soil slightly moist. Do not overwater. Begonia roots rot easily in excessive moisture. Maximum humidity is necessary for rex begonia. If room conditions are excessively dry, place containers in a pan of pebbles or gravel filled with water. Night temperatures should be 60° to 65° and day temperatures 65° to 75°.

Fertilize established plants monthly from February until November. Do not feed newly potted or repotted plants for at least 2 months. Repot crowded plants during the spring.

Move potted begonias outdoors for the summer

Angelwing begonia (*B. coccinea*)

and sink the pots in the ground in a partially shaded location. A shaded porch or balcony will be sufficient if outside garden space is unavailable.

Propagate rex begonias by leaf or stem cuttings at any time of the year. Cut wedges of leaves along main veins and root the cuttings in sand.

Rex begonia (*Begonia* x *rex-cultorum*)

Caladium *(C. hortulanum)*

Caladium

Caladiums *(C. hortulanum)* are among the most colorful of foliage houseplants. Leaves are large and shaped like arrowheads. Most selections have bicolored leaves: pink or red with sharp, green veins. A number of selections are also available with variegated foliage. Caladium leaves are 6 to 24 inches long.

Caladiums are tuberous plants with leaves arising from the base. The plant grows during the spring and summer, then enters a period of dormancy in late fall and winter when the leaves wither and die. New growth begins in the spring.

Locate caladiums in medium light. During the summer, bring plants outdoors and give them a partially shaded place. When using artificial light indoors, provide 400 to 500 footcandles.

Grow caladiums in peaty soil (2 parts peat moss or leaf mold to 1 part garden loam and 1 part sand). Keep the soil moist during spring and summer while the plant is growing. Beginning in mid-October, gradually reduce the frequency of watering, then begin to reduce the amount of water distributed each time. In late fall, snip off the dead foliage and store pots in a cool place at 60° to 65°. Do not water while plants are dormant.

Caladiums prefer high humidity. Young plants should be kept warm, 75° to 80°, and established plants should be kept at 65° to 70°.

Fertilize caladiums every month during the growing season. After the foliage has browned, begin to reduce the dosage of fertilizer until the foliage withers and dies.

Repot dormant tubers (roots) in early spring. Divide tubers and pot them individually to increase plants. Remove newly repotted bulbs to medium light and resume watering. Begin fertilizing new plants 1 month after growth begins.

Cast-iron plant

Some plant names describe the nature of a plant rather than its appearance. Cast-iron plant *(Aspidistra elatior)* is nearly indestructible; it tolerates heat, low light, and dry, dusty conditions better than most, if not all, other house plants. Aspidistra seems to thrive on partial neglect, but performs exceptionally well when given proper care and location. The cast-iron plant heads the list of plants recommended for beginners and for pessimists who are convinced that they cannot grow anything.

Mature plants are 2 to 3 feet tall with dark green, oblong-elliptic leaves which may grow 18 to 30

Cast-iron plant (*Aspidistra elatior*)

cellent plant for rooms with subdued light, such as bathrooms and bedrooms. It is attractive alone, or it can add height and dimension to the mixed planter. The 6- to 10-inch leaves are ovate and borne singly at the end of each canelike stem. The variety 'White Rajah' has variegated foliage.

Locate Chinese evergreen in medium or low light. If artificial light is used, provide 50 to 150 footcandles. Direct sun will scorch the leaves.

Soil for Chinese evergreen should be peaty loam (equal parts potting soil, perlite, and peat moss). Or grow Chinese evergreen in water alone. If you use a soil medium, keep the soil moist at all times. Provide medium humidity. Chinese evergreen prefers a temperature range of 65 to 70 degrees at night and 70 to 85 during the day.

Fertilize established plants monthly. Wait at least 2 months before feeding newly potted or repotted plants. Repotting can be done during any season.

Propagate Chinese evergreen at any time of the year from stem cuttings or by dividing the roots at repotting time. To keep plants attractive, occasional pruning will be necessary. Snip off leaf stems 2 inches beneath the base of the leaf and root these in water or moist sand.

inches long and 4 inches wide. *Aspidistra elatior* Variegata has green leaves with strips of white running lengthwise.

Locate aspidistra in medium to low light. Rooms with subdued lighting, such as bedrooms and bathrooms, are excellent places for aspidistra. When using artificial lighting, provide at least 150 footcandles.

Soil for aspidistra should be loamy. Although the cast-iron plant is fairly drought-resistant, best growth results when soil is kept slightly moist at all times. Provide medium to low humidity and a temperature range of 50° to 60° at night and 65° to 75° during the day.

Fertilize established plants every 2 months during the spring, summer, and fall, but withhold fertilizer during the winter. Do not fertilize newly potted or repotted plants for at least 2 months. Repot crowded plants in early spring or whenever repotting becomes necessary.

Propagate the cast-iron plant in spring by dividing the roots.

Chinese evergreen

Among the easiest house plants to grow is the Chinese evergreen (*Aglaonema sp.*). Its light and cultural requirements are suited to conditions found in most homes. Chinese evergreen is an ex-

Chinese evergreen (*Aglaonema sp.*)

Common coleus (*C. blumei*)

Coleus

Common coleus (*C. blumei*) is a medium-size plant with small to medium leaves brightly colored and marked. Coleus is a popular annual bedding plant in many areas of the country in addition to being a widely grown house plant. Native to Java, the 2- to 4-inch red, green, or yellow foliage of coleus is a welcome addition to either home or garden. Standard or tree form varieties are also available.

Locate coleus in a sunny window where it will receive 4 or 5 hours of direct sunlight each day or in a light room where indirect sun is bright during most of the day. When using only artificial light, provide at least 500 to 1200 footcandles.

Plant coleus in loamy potting soil and keep the soil moist. Coleus likes moderate humidity and a temperature range of 60° to 70° at night and 70° to 85° during the day.

Fertilize established plants monthly. Wait at least 2 months before feeding newly potted or repotted plants. Repot coleus annually at any time of the year.

To stimulate branching and produce bushy plants, pinch out the tips of stems. This will also keep plants compact. Remove flower buds as they form.

Common coleus can be grown from seed or from stem cuttings taken at any time of the year.

Coleus is most effectively displayed in masses on tables or shelves.

Croton

Croton (*Codiaeum variegatum* Pictum) is a medium-size plant with long, lobed or twisted leaves, 12 to 18 inches long. Leaf colors include green, bronze, yellow, red, pink, and white. Croton leaves are often multicolored. Native to the South Pacific islands, crotons are grown as 6- to 10-foot shrubs in their native habitat. Inconspicuous flowers

Codiaeum variegatum Pictum, *C. variegatum* 'The Queen', *C. variegatum* 'Baron Rothschild'

are borne on drooping racemes.

Locate crotons in bright rooms where they will receive at least 4 to 5 hours of sunlight each day. When using artificial lighting, provide 500 to 1200 footcandles.

Pot crotons in loamy soil and keep the soil moist. Moderate humidity with a temperature range of 65° to 70° at night and 70° to 85° during the day is best for crotons. Avoid drafts or the leaves may drop.

Feed crotons monthly from March through July, but withhold fertilizer during the rest of the year. Do not feed newly potted or repotted plants for at least 2 months. Repot crotons annually during spring.

Crotons are vigorous growers and must be pruned to be attractive. A croton, left unpruned, may become 6 feet tall in 3 years. Pruning should be done in early spring.

Propagate crotons by stem cuttings taken in spring or by air-layering. Plants that become leggy can be reduced in size by air-layering. Layer the top of the plant 3 or 4 inches below the lowest leaves, then cut the top from the old plant and pot as a new plant.

Dieffenbachia

Dieffenbachias (*D. amoena, D. picta*) are popular house plants grown for their large, variegated foliage. *D. amoena* has 14- to 20-inch dark green leaves with white markings along the veins. *D. picta* has dark green leaves spotted white. The variety 'Rudolph Roehrs' has 8- to 12-inch yellow green leaves blotched with ivory and edged in green. Native to the American tropics, dieffenbachias are excellent as specimens or grouped with other plants in a large planter.

Two cautions: Dieffenbachia sap is toxic in open cuts. Be careful when removing leaves or cutting the cane. In addition, chewing on parts of the plant causes temporary loss of speech, hence the common name, dumb cane.

Dieffenbachia (*D. amoena*)

Locate dieffenbachia in medium to full light. When using artificial lighting, provide 200 to 500 footcandles.

Soil for dieffenbachias should be loamy. Allow soil to become a little dry between waterings, then water thoroughly. Overwatering is very harmful to dieffenbachia, causing the roots and canes to rot. Temperature range should be 65° to 70° at night and 70° to 80° during the day. Low humidity is best for dieffenbachia.

Fertilize established plants lightly each month. In-sufficient fertilization may cause lower leaves to drop. Do not fertilize newly potted or repotted plants for at least 2 months. Repot crowded plants at any time of the year.

Prune plants to keep them low and attractive. As bottom leaves age and yellow, remove them. If too much of the lower stem becomes bare, cut off the top of the plant and root it in sand or water. Keep the canes; they eventually grow lateral shoots.

Propagate dieffenbachia at any time of the year by stem cuttings rooted in sphagnum moss or by air-layering.

Dracaena

Several species of dracaena are popular house plants. The foliage and growth habits of these are so varied that it is difficult to believe they are all members of the same genus. *Dracaena godseffiana* is a 2- to 3-foot multistemmed plant with elliptic, flat green leaves with cream specks. *D. fragrans,* perhaps the best known species, has 18- to 32-inch leaves that arch gracefully away from a single stalk. Leaves are green with a gold band down the middle. *D. sanderiana* is usually smaller than the others, with gray green leaves bordered in white; but even this species is capable of growing 4 to 5 feet tall.

Locate dracaenas in medium light. If artificial lighting is used, provide 50 to 150 footcandles.

Soil for dracaenas should be loamy but well drained so that roots do not stand in water. Keep

Dracaenas; Left: *D. sanderiana.* Right: *D. fragrans.*

English ivy (*Hedera helix*)

soil as moist as possible without allowing water to collect in the drainage saucer beneath the pot. Dracaenas prefer low humidity and warm temperatures, 65° to 70° at night, 70° to 85° during the day.

Fertilize established plants monthly. Hold off on feeding newly potted or repotted plants for at least 2 months. Repot crowded plants at any time of the year.

To keep plants looking their best, wash the foliage monthly with soapy water, but do not allow soapy water to spill onto the soil; most household detergents contain phosphate compounds which promote the growth of algae. If the bottom part of the stem becomes leggy and bare, cut off the leafy portion and root it like a stem cutting. Cut the remaining bare stem into 3- to 4-inch sections and lay them horizontally in rooting medium. Shoots and roots will develop along each segment.

Propagate dracaenas at any time by stem cuttings or by air-layering.

English Ivy

English ivy (*Hedera helix*) is a climbing or trailing plant with medium to small green or variegated leathery leaves. A native of Europe, English ivy has been widely naturalized throughout the United States. As an indoor plant, it ranks high on the list of easy-to-grow foliage plants.

English ivy will tolerate a wide range of light conditions, from low-medium to full light, if the acclimatization to full light is gradual. When using artificial light, provide at least 400 foot-candles.

Grow English ivy in loamy potting soil. Keep the soil moderately moist and provide humidity by placing the pot on a tray of pebbles barely covered with water. English ivy prefers a cool location with night temperatures of 50 to 60 degrees and day temperatures of 60 to 70 degrees.

Fertilize established plants monthly (twice a month in summer) with a mild liquid fertilizer. Do not feed newly potted or repotted plants for at least 2 months. Repot English ivy annually or as plants become crowded. Repot at any time of the year.

Propagate English ivy from stem cuttings at any time. Plants will be bushier if the tips of stems are pinched out. These cuttings may then be rooted.

Display English ivy on a pole or piece of driftwood that the vines can climb, or place containers in an elevated position from which plants may cascade. English ivy is especially suited for hanging baskets. Small leaved varieties are also used in terrariums.

Fig, Rubber plant

Plants of the genus *Ficus* are among the most varied and interesting low maintenance plants for indoor gardeners. Included in this genus are weeping fig (*Ficus benjamina*), rubber plant (*F. elastica*), fiddle-leaf fig (*F. lyrata*), and the common fig (*F. carica*).

Weeping fig (*Ficus benjamina*)

Rubber plant *(Ficus elastica)*

Weeping fig is a tall, treelike house plant with small, glossy leaves that droop. Rubber plant, which may reach 8 to 10 feet at maturity, has large, ovate leaves. Fiddle-leaf fig resembles rubber plant in form and leaf size, but the leaves are more obovate and flatter at the tips. Common fig is not often grown as an indoor plant. However, given optimum growing conditions, figs have been grown in tubs and have borne fruit as far north as Boston.

The rubber plant is one of the most popular house plants sold in America. Because *Ficus* adapts well to a wide range of growing conditions, figs and rubber plants are often found in stores and offices as well as homes.

Locate *Ficus* in medium light. When using artificial lighting, provide 200 to 500 footcandles.

Soil should be loamy and kept slightly moist. Provide medium humidity and a temperature range of 65° to 70° at night and 70° to 85° during the day.

Fertilize established plants every month. Do not feed newly potted or repotted plants for at least 2 months. *Ficus* grows best when the roots are somewhat crowded. Do not repot unless new growth is stunted and weak and roots are excessively crowded, as may be evidenced by their protruding through the drainage hole in the bottom of the pot. When repotting becomes necessary, it is best done in the spring.

To maintain their glossy appearance, wipe the leaves frequently with a damp cloth. If leaves begin to drop and a great portion of the stem is left unattractively bare, air-layer the top portion and pot it as a new plant. This may be done at any time of the year. In spring, cut the old stalk back to within a few inches of the soil. The old plant will soon begin to produce new growth.

Propagate *Ficus* by air-layering or by stem cuttings.

Grape Ivy

Grape ivy (*Cissus rhombifolia*) is a climbing or trailing plant with angled stems and medium-size compound leaves composed of 3 sharp-toothed oval leaflets. Native to northern South America, grape ivy has for years been a popular house plant in the United States. It is also known as Venezuela treebine.

Locate grape ivy in medium to bright light. When using artificial light, provide at least 400 footcandles.

A loamy potting soil is best for grape ivy. Keep the soil slightly moist. Like other ivies, grape ivy likes cool night temperatures, between 50° and 55°, and day temperatures of 65° to 70°. Low to medium humidity will produce the best growth results.

Fertilize established plants monthly. Wait at least

Grape ivy (*Cissus rhombifolia*)

69

2 months before fertilizing newly potted or repotted plants. Overcrowded plants may be repotted at any time of the year.

Pinch off tips of stems to encourage branching and bushy growth. This may be done at any time. Use these stem cuttings to root new plants.

Grape ivy can be grown on poles or other supports for vines. It is also well suited for hanging baskets or for cascading from a mantle or high shelf.

Monstera

Monstera (*M. deliciosa*) is a large, vining plant with waxy, heart-shaped leaves which are split and perforated. As potted house plants, monsteras grow from 2 to 5 feet tall and may require staking or other support. In their native Central American habitat, these plants are straggly climbers with leaves up to 3

Monstera (*M. deliciosa*), also called Splitleaf philodendron, Swiss cheese plant, and Hurricane plant.

feet long and edible fruit. Other popular names for monstera include split-leaf philodendron, cutleaf philodendron, Swiss cheese plant, hurricane plant, and ceriman. Immature forms of monstera, with the large, young leaves unsplit, are botanically classed as *Philodendron pertusum*.

Locate monstera in medium-low to medium-high light, but not in direct sunlight. Medium-high light and fertilization will increase the size of the leaves and the number of splits. When using artificial light, provide at least 400 footcandles.

Monstera thrives in a soil mix of peaty loam. Mix 1 part garden loam, 1 part sharp sand, and 2 parts peat moss or leaf mold. Keep soil moist to medium dry. Provide night temperatures of 65° to 70° and day temperatures of 70° to 80°. Support, such as a pole or moss stick, may be necessary.

Fertilize established plants in March and in June. Hold off on fertilizing new plants or newly repotted plants for 2 months. Overcrowded plants may be repotted at any time of the year. Large air roots are normal and can be removed if they become unsightly.

Propagate monstera from seeds, stem cuttings, or by air-layering. Propagation may be done at any time.

Peperomia

Peperomia (*Peperomia obtusifolia*) is a medium-low, bushy plant with wrinkled, reddish stems and alternate, oblanceolate leaves, 4 inches long and 2 to 3 inches wide. Selections are available with a red margin around the leaves and with cream-colored markings. A related species called watermelon peperomia (*P. argyreia*) bears its leaves in rosettes. The fleshy leaves are dark green to bluish and have bands of silver radiating from their upper centers. Peperomias are especially valuable for their tolerance of varying growing conditions, including partial neglect.

Locate peperomias in medium to bright indirect sunlight. When using only artificial lighting, provide 200 to 500 footcandles.

Pot peperomias in peaty loam. A mix of 1 part garden loam, 1 part sharp sand (or perlite), and 2 parts peat moss is an excellent potting soil for peperomia. Allow soil to become moderately dry between waterings, then water thoroughly. Overwatering will soon kill peperomias. Ideal temperatures for peperomia are 65° to 70° at night, 75° to 80° during the day.

Wait at least 2 months to fertilize newly potted or repotted plants, but feed established plants *every* month. Repotting is rarely required, but may be-

Peperomias; Left: *P. obtusifolia.* Top: *P. scandens* Variegata. Bottom: *P. caperata.*

come necessary every few years. Repot peperomia in early spring when new growth begins.

Propagate peperomias by stem or leaf cuttings taken at any time of the year.

Philodendron

Philodendrons are the most popular house plants in the United States. So varied are they from species to species that a small room could be decorated with philodendrons alone. Among the most favored species are: heart-leaf philodendron *(Philodendron cordatum),* spade-leaf philodendron *(P. domesticum),* velvet-leaf philodendron *(P. scandens),* saddle-leaf philodendron *(P. selloum),* fiddle-leaf philodendron *(P. bipennifolium),* and Wendland's philodendron *(P. wendlandii).* In addition to these, monstera *(Monstera deliciosa)* is closely related to the philodendrons. All are native to the American tropics.

Heart-leaf philodendron is a trailing or climbing vine with small, glossy, heart-shaped leaves. It combines well with other plants in a mixed planter or in a hanging basket. Displayed by itself, heart-leaf philodendron will cascade from an elevated shelf or, given a moss stick or other support, it will climb.

Spade-leaf philodendron, also called spear-head

philodendron, has large, glossy, spade-shaped leaves. A similar plant with reddish leaves and stems is called Burgundy philodendron. Like other philodendrons, these two may be trained to grow on a trellis, a pole, or a large moss stick.

Philodendrons adapt to a wide range of light from medium-low to medium-high, but do not locate them in direct sunlight. When using artificial light, provide at least 50 to 150 footcandles.

Soil should be loamy to peaty. Most philodendrons will also grow in sphagnum moss. Keep potting medium moist. Philodendrons grow best in low humidity and a temperature range of 65° to 70° at night and 70° to 85° during the day.

Fertilize established plants every 2 to 4 months but do not feed newly potted or repotted plants for at least 2 months. Repotting can be done at any time of the year.

Wash philodendron leaves once a month with soap and water to maintain their glossy appearance.

When plants grow to the end of their supporting trellis or moss stick, cut the stems back about 6 inches from the top to promote new branching.

Propagate spade-leaf philodendron by stem cutting cuttings (these will form roots in water) or by air layering; propagation may be done at any time of the year.

Heart-leaf philodendron *(P. cordatum)*

Piggyback plant (*Tolmiea menziesii*)

Piggyback plant

Among those house plants that delight but do not demand is the piggyback (or pick-a-back) plant (*Tolmiea menziesii*). The common name is derived from this plant's unique method of reproduction. Tiny plantlets are borne at the base of the mature leaf blades and give the appearance of riding piggyback on the mother plant. Native to western Canada and the United States, piggyback plant is a small- to medium-size plant with hairy, lobed leaves.

Locate piggyback plant in medium to full light. If artificial lighting is used, provide 200 to 500 footcandles.

Soil should be loamy and well drained, although piggyback plants are more tolerant of wet soil than most other house plants. Keep soil moist at all times. Temperatures should be cool, 50° to 60° at night, 60° to 70° during the day. Provide high humidity by placing potted plants on a tray filled with pebbles nearly covered with water.

Fertilize established plants every month. Withhold fertilizer from newly potted or repotted plants for at least 2 months. Repot overcrowded piggyback plants at any time of the year.

Propagation can be done at any time of year from cuttings of leaves bearing plantlets. Make cuttings with about 2 inches of leaf stem and insert the stem in moist sand or perlite with the base of the leaf resting on the rooting medium.

Prayer Plant

Prayer plants (*Maranta bicolor, M. leuconeura*) are small plants with obovate leaves 6 inches long and 3 to 4 inches wide. Leaves of *M. bicolor* have dark green to mahogany spots with light purple un-

dersides. Leaves of *M. leuconeura* are light green, spotted along the midrib, and purple underneath; leaf veins are fine and have a silken sheen. Native to Brazil, these curious plants fold up their leaves in the absence of light, giving the impression of hands folded in prayer, hence the common name.

Locate maranta in medium to bright indirect light. When using artificial light, provide 200 to 500 footcandles.

Prayer plants prefer loamy potting soil which is kept medium moist. Be certain that containers are well drained. Although prayer plants like moist soil, water allowed to stand around the top of the rootball or the stems may cause rot. Because marantas require high humidity, they are ideally placed in a bathroom or over a kitchen sink. Provide night temperatures of 65° to 70° and day temperatures of 70° to 80°.

Fertilize established plants once in summer and once in early fall. Do not feed newly potted or repotted plants for at least 2 months. Repot marantas annually during the early spring.

Propagate prayer plants in early spring while repotting them. Divide the clumps of roots and repot divisions individually.

Prayer plant (*Maranta leuconeura*)

Schefflera

Scheffleras (*Brassaia actinophylla*) are large, upright plants that may grow to 6 or 7 feet at maturity. In their native Australian habitat, scheffleras can grow to 40 feet and are commonly called umbrella trees or octopus trees. The smooth, evergreen leaves grow out radially from the end of each stalk,

Schefflera (*Brassaia actinophylla*)

giving each stem an umbrellalike effect. Mature leaves may be up to 12 inches long. As a long-lived, undemanding house plant, schefflera rates high.

Locate scheffleras in a sunny window where they will get at least 4 or 5 hours of direct sunlight each day or in a bright room with light walls. Scheffleras also respond well to artificial lighting. Avoid drafty locations.

Allow the soil to become nearly dry between thorough waterings. Daily misting is not necessary, but scheffleras do respond well to misting once or twice a week. Night temperatures of 60° to 70° and day temperatures of 70° to 85° are ideal for scheffleras.

Feed scheffleras twice a year: at annual repotting, then again 6 months later. Repot them at any time of the year. Mix equal parts of loam, peat moss, and sand (or perlite), then add 1 tablespoon of complete fertilizer per gallon of soil mix. Repot schefflera in this medium. Six months later, top-dress with 1 tablespoon of complete fertilizer. Because feeding of scheffleras is infrequent, slow-release fertilizers are recommended.

Propagate scheffleras from seeds or from cuttings.

Snake plant

Snake plants (*Sansevieria zeylanica, S. trifasciata* Laurentii) are upright plants, growing in clumps of heavy, swordlike vertical leaves 18 to 32 inches long. *S. zeylanica* has dark green, mottled leaves and *S. trifasciata* Laurentii has similar leaves with a cream-white margin. A dwarf species, *S. trifasciata* Hahnii, has wider leaves that grow only 4 to 6 inches long. Other common names include mother-in-law tongue and bowstring hemp. They are native to Africa and Ceylon.

Locate sansevierias in low to medium-high light. When using artificial light, provide at least 50 to 150 footcandles. They prefer loamy soil which is kept medium moist to dry. Water less during winter when the plant is dormant—just enough to keep the plant from shriveling. Temperatures should be 60 to 70 degrees at night and 75 to 80 degrees during the day.

Sansevierias are useful for their height and form in mixed plantings. They are noted for their durability under adverse growing conditions, including negligence and low humidity.

Feed lightly every 2 or 3 months during spring, summer, and early fall. Do not fertilize during winter. Repot every 4 or 5 years at any time of the year. Do not feed newly potted or repotted plants for at least 2 months.

Propagate sansevieria by dividing the clumps or by rooting 4-inch leaf cuttings. When *S. trifasciata* Laurentii is propagated by division, it continues to produce striped leaves, but when propagated by leaf cuttings, it produces plain green leaves. Propagation may be done at any time of the year.

Snake plant (*Sansevieria trifasciata*)

Spider plant (*Chlorophytum comosum*), also called Airplane plant.

Spider plant

Spider plant (*Chlorophytum comosum*) is a popular plant for hanging containers with long, grasslike leaves that arch and curl away from the container like the legs of a spider. Leaves of mature plants are 12 to 16 inches long and green with a greenish white band along the middle. The roots also send out long, wiry stems or runners that bear either flowers or new plants. Native to South Africa, spider plants are very easy to grow and can survive neglect better than most houseplants.

Locate spider plants in medium to full light, though it is wise to place them in partial or filtered shade when moving them outdoors for the summer. Provide 200 to 500 footcandles when using artificial light.

Soil for spider plants should be loamy and kept moist. Ideal temperatures are 50° to 60° at night and 65° to 75° during the day. Medium humidity is best for spider plants.

Fertilize established plants every 3 or 4 months, but do not fertilize newly potted or repotted plants for at least 4 to 6 months. Repotting is usually not necessary for several years. When necessary, however, repotting can be done at any time of the year.

Aside from hanging containers, spider plants are also effectively displayed on shelves where leaves and runners may trail.

Propagate spider plants at any time by snipping plantlets from the runners when the aerial roots are ¼ inch long and potting each plantlet individually.

Swedish ivy

Swedish ivy (*Plectranthus australis*) is a trailing, vinelike plant that seldom becomes straggly and unkempt as may happen with the more common ivies. The medium-size cordate to orbicular leaves are green or variegated with white margins. Swedish ivy can be pinched frequently to maintain a full, compact growth habit for pots, or it can be allowed to trail and form handsome specimen for an elevated shelf or hanging basket. Leaf and stem surfaces have a moist, waxy appearance and look good with gourds and other decorative fruits.

Locate Swedish ivy in bright light. A sunny room is ideal, but avoid prolonged direct sunlight as this

Variegated Swedish ivy (*Plectranthus australis* Variegata)

may cause wilting. When using artificial light, provide 400 to 500 footcandles.

Soil for Swedish ivy should be loamy and kept slightly moist. Provide medium humidity and cool temperatures, 55° to 65° at night and 70° to 75° during the day.

Fertilize established plants every two months, but do not feed newly potted or repotted plants for at least 2 months. Overcrowded plants may be repotted at any time of the year.

Propagate Swedish ivy from stem cuttings taken at any time or by dividing the roots at repotting time. Stem cuttings may not reproduce foliage variegation, but divisions will. Stem cuttings can be rooted in water or in moist sand or perlite.

Wandering Jew

Few vinelike plants exhibit more vitality than a wandering Jew. The farther these vigorous plants spread, the more exciting their effect. Wandering Jews are excellent trailing from a shelf, though they are most often displayed in hanging baskets.

Three species of plants belonging tc the spiderwort family are popularly called wandering Jew: *Zebrina pendula, Tradescantia fluminensis,* and *Gibasis geniculata.* All are trailing, vinelike plants with plain green or variegated green and white or purple silver leaves.

The main characteristic that distinguishes the species from one another is the color of their inconspicuous flowers; those of *Zebrina* are purple and those of *Tradescantia* are white. The leaves of *Zebrina* are also tinted purple. All wandering Jews are easy to grow.

Gibasis geniculata, also called Tahitian bridal veil, is frequently referred to as a wandering Jew. The leaves do resemble those of *Zebrina* and *Tradescantia,* though they are much smaller than those of the more common types of wandering Jew. In general, the culture of *Gibasis* is the same as that of other wandering Jews.

Locate wandering Jews in medium to full light. If artificial lighting is used, provide 200 to 500 footcandles.

Soil for wandering Jew should be loamy and kept medium-moist. Wandering Jews grow best in medium humidity and a temperature range of 65 to 70 degrees at night and 70 to 85 degrees in the daytime.

Feed established plants every 2 months but do not fertilize newly potted or repotted plants for at least 3 months. Repotting may be done at any time of the year.

Propagate wandering Jews at any time from stem cuttings. Root them first in sand or water, or plant the cuttings directly in small pots.

Wandering Jew (*Tradescantia fluminensis*)

FOLIAGE HOUSE PLANTS

Latin name	Common names	Watering	Light	Temp.	Humidity	Repotting soil
Adiantum sp.	Maidenhair fern	growing season moist at all times; dry in winter	low	50°–70°	high	loamy plus fir bark
Agave americana	Century plant	dry between waterings; 2–3 weeks in winter	4 hrs. DS/day	50°–70°	medium	loamy plus charcoal
Aglaonema sp.	Chinese evergreen, see page 64					
Aloe vera	Aloe / Burn plant	dry between thorough waterings	4 hrs. DS/day	50°–70°	medium	loamy plus charcoal
Araucaria heterophylla	Norfolk Island pine	barely moist all the time	FS; DS winter	45°–80°	medium	sandy peat, sandy loam
Asparagus sprengeri / A. setaceus	Asparagus fern, see page 61					
Aspidistra elatior	Cast-iron plant, see page 63					
Asplenium sp.	Spleenwort / Bird's-nest fern / Mother fern	always moist spring to fall; barely moist in winter	low	50°–70°	high	loamy plus fir bark
Aucuba japonica / A. japonica Variegata	Japanese aucuba / Gold dust plant	barely moist all the time	medium	40°–65°	high	loamy
Beaucarnea recurvata	Elephant-foot tree	dry between thorough waterings	DS or FS	50°–70°	medium	loamy
Begonia x rex-cultorum	Rex begonia, see page 62					
Brassaia actinophylla	Schefflera, see page 72 / Queensland umbrella tree					
Caladium hortulanum	Caladium, see page 63					
Calathea makoyana	Peacock plant	moist all the time	medium	65°–85°	high	sandy plus peat
Cephalocereus senilis	Old man cactus	dry between waterings spring to fall; 2–3 weeks in winter	4 hrs. DS/day	65°–85°; 40°–60° winter	low	sandy plus charcoal
Chamaedorea elegans	Parlor palm	moist all the time	low	65°–85°	medium	loamy
Chamaedorea erumpens	Bamboo palm	moist all the time	low	65°–85°	medium	loamy
Chlorophytum comosum	Spider plant, see page 74 / Airplane plant					
Cissus rhombifolia	Grape ivy, see page 69					
Codiaeum variegatum	Croton, see page 65					
Coleus blumei	Common coleus, see page 65					

Latin name	Common names	Watering	Light	Temp.	Humidity	Repotting soil
Cordyline terminalis	Hawaiian ti plant	moist all the time	4 hrs. DS/day	65°–85°	high	loamy
Dieffenbachia sp.	Dieffenbachia, see page 66 Dumb cane					
Dracaena sp.	Dracaena, see page 67 Corn plant					
Echeveria sp.	Painted lady Mexican snowball Plush plant	dry between thorough waterings spring to fall; 2-3 weeks in winter	4 hrs. DS; FS	50°–70°		
Epipremnum aureum	Devil's ivy	dry between thorough waterings	medium	65°–85°	medium	loamy or water
Euonymus sp.	Evergreen euonymus Winter creeper	barely moist all the time	medium	40°–70°	medium	loamy
Fatsia japonica	Japanese aralia	barely moist all the time	4 hrs. DS/day	40°–65°	medium	loamy
Ficus sp.	Rubber plant, see page 68 Weeping fig Fiddle-leaf fig Indian laurel					
Fittonia sp.	Fittonia Mosaic plant	moist all the time	low to medium	65°–85°	high	loamy
Gibasis geniculata	Tahitian bridal veil, see page 75					
Gynura aurantiaca Sarmentosa	Purple passion vine	barely moist all the time	FS; best in 4 hrs. DS/day	65°–85°	medium	loamy
Haworthia sp.	Haworthia Star cactus	fairly dry between thorough waterings	medium	50°–70°	medium	loamy plus charcoal
Hedera helix	English ivy, see page 68					
Howea forsterana	Sentry palm Kentia palm	barely moist all the time	medium	60°–85°	medium	loamy plus peat
Mammillaria sp.	Bird's-nest cactus Golden star cactus Old lady cactus	dry between thorough waterings; 2-3 weeks in winter	FS; best in 4 hrs. DS/day	65°–85° 40°–65° winter	low	sandy loam plus charcoal
Maranta leuconeura	Prayer plant, see page 72					
Monstera deliciosa	Split-leaf philodendron, see page 70 Cut-leaf philodendron Swiss cheese plant Hurricane plant					

FOLIAGE HOUSE PLANTS

Latin name	Common names	Watering	Light	Temp.	Humidity	Repotting soil
Nephrolepis exaltata Bostoniensis	Boston fern	barely moist all the time	medium	50°–70°	medium	loamy plus fir bark
Notocactus sp.	Golden ball cactus Silver ball cactus Sun cup	dry between thorough waterings; 2–3 weeks in winter	4 hrs. DS/day	65°–85°. 40°–65° winter	low	sandy loam plus charcoal
Opuntia sp.	Beaver-tail cactus Paper-spined pear cactus Bunny-ears	dry between thorough waterings; 2–3 weeks in winter	4 hrs. DS/day	65°–85°. 40°–65° winter	low	sandy loam plus charcoal
Osmanthus heterophyllus	Holly olive	barely moist all the time	4 hrs. DS/day	40°–75°	medium	loamy
Pachyphytum oviferum	Moonstones Sugared almonds	dry between thorough waterings; 2–3 weeks in winter	FS; DS 4 hrs. is best	50°–70°	low	sandy loam plus charcoal
Pandanus veitchii	Screwpine	fairly dry between thorough waterings	FS or medium	65°–85°	medium	loamy
Peperomia sp.	Silver dollar, see page 70 Pepper face Watermelon peperomia					
Philodendron sp.	Heart-leaf philodendron, see page 71 Spade-leaf philodendron Saddle-leaf philodendron					
Pilea sp.	Aluminum plant, see page 60 Artillery plant Panamiga					
Pittosporum tobira	Japanese pittosporum	fairly dry between thorough waterings	4 hrs. DS; FS	40°–80°	medium	loamy
Platycerium bifurcatum	Staghorn fern	moist all the time	medium	50°–70°	medium	sphagnum moss
Plectranthus australis	Swedish ivy, see page 74					
Podocarpus macrophyllus Maki	Japanese yew	barely moist all the time	4 hrs. DS; FS	40°–85°	medium	loamy
Polypodium aureum	Rabbit's-foot fern Golden polypody	barely moist all the time	low	50°–85°	medium	loamy plus fir bark
Polyscias sp.	Aralia	barely moist all the time	FS; DS is best	65°–85°	high	loamy
Pteris sp.	Brake fern Cretan brake fern Victoria fern	barely moist all the time	low	50°–70°	medium	loamy plus fir bark

78

Latin name	Common names	Watering	Light	Temp.	Humidity	Repotting soil
Rhoeo spathacea	Moses-in-the-cradle	barely moist all the time	medium	50°–70°	medium	loamy
Sansevieria sp.	Snake plant, see page 73 Mother-in-law tongue					
Sedum morganianum	Burro's-tail Donkey's-tail	dry between thorough waterings, 2–3 weeks in winter	FS; best in 4 hrs. DS/day	50°–70°	low	sandy loam plus charcoal
Soleirolia soleirolii	Baby's-tears, see page 61					
Syngonium podophyllum	Arrowhead vine Syngonium, nephthytis African evergreen	slightly moist at all times	medium	65°–85°	medium	loamy
Tolmiea menziesii	Piggyback plant, see page 72					
Tradescantia fluminensis	Wandering Jew, see page 75					
Zebrina pendula	Wandering Jew, see page 75					

Watering: Moist in this context means do not soak. A plant that should be moist at all times should never be wet and never be dry.

Cactus and other succulents use very little water in winter. Use only enough to keep them from shriveling; about 2 to 3 weeks between waterings.

Light: DS means direct sunlight, usually at least 4 hours daily. FS means filtered sunlight or a bright room Medium can often be found in north or east facing windows. Low light means the plant will tolerate very little light, but in most cases would prefer more.

Temperature: The lowest temperature listed is the coolest nighttime temperature recommended and the higher one is the highest recommended daytime temperature. Somewhere between the two should suit your home.

Humidity: Low and medium mean the conditions found in most homes. High means place the plants on a tray of pebbles filled nearly to the top of the pebbles with water. Misting the plants daily is also recommended.

Repotting soil: Loamy means equal parts garden loam, peat moss, and sand or perlite. Leaf mold and finely ground compost are good substitutes for peat moss. Sandy loam means 2 parts sand or perlite to 1 part loam and 1 part peat moss. Peaty soil is rich in organic matter, composed of 1 part sand, 1 part loam, and 2 parts peat.

Favorite Flowering Plants

African Violet

African violets (*Saintpaulia* sp.) can bloom year-round if given the proper care and environment. Although African violets are easy to grow, they are not always easy to bloom. Despite this fact, they continue to be the most popular flowering house plant in America.

The selection of flower colors is quite varied and many are easy to find at local garden centers. The following is a list of some of the most popular double- and single-flowering varieties:

Doubles and Semi-Doubles	*Singles and Semi-Doubles*
Blue	**Blue and Purple**
'Montania Blue'	'Blue Revery'
'Countdown'	'Diania Englert Blue'
'Duet'	'Memories'
Purple	**White**
'Rhapsodie Elfreide'	'Silver Dollar'
'Dapper Dan'	'Butterfly White'
'Alakazam'	'Moon Drop'
Orchid and Lavender	**Pink**
'Dancer'	'Lieberman Sport'
'Wings of Beauty'	'Fanfare'
'Floral Fantasy'	'Rhapsodie Claudia'
White	**Red**
'Sea Foam'	'Mr. R.'
'Platinum'	'Hi Fi'
'Tommy Lou'	'Diania Englert Red'
Pink	**Orchid and Lavender**
'Moderne Jewel'	'Tipt'
'Beau Catcher'	'Milwaukee'
'Candlewick'	'Spinner'
Red	
'Melanie'	
'Baroness'	
'Red Sparkle'	

Locate African violets in bright, indirect light, but not direct sunlight. When growing them under artificial lights (to which African violets respond well), provide at least 200 to 500 footcandles.

Soil for African violets should be loamy and well drained. Keep the soil barely moist at all times. It is best to water African violets by subirrigating or by *double potting* (see Chapter Two *Watering House Plants*). Temperatures should range from 65° to 70° at night and 70° to 85° in the daytime. In warm places, increase humidity by placing containers on a tray of pebbles filled nearly to the top of the pebbles with water. The cooler the plants are kept, the less humidity they require.

Fertilize established plants every month. Do not fertilize newly potted plants for at least 1 month. Repot African violets in late spring or early summer. In repotting them, keep the crowns slightly above soil level.

Insects that are fond of African violets include aphids, cyclamen mites, mealybugs, leaf miners, and sowbugs. Segregate infested plants im-

African violet (*Saintpaulia* sp.)

Azalea *(Azalea sp.)*

mediately and apply appropriate control measures (see Chapter Four, *Curing Plant Ailments*.)

Propagate African violets from divisions, from leaf cuttings, or from leaf petiole (leaf plus its stem) cuttings.

Azalea

Among the most popular of evergreen outdoor shrubs, azaleas *(Azalea sp.)* are also favorite container plants and adapt easily to indoor culture. With their delicate, weeping stamens and bell-shaped blossoms, azaleas are spectacular gift plants, especially around Valentine's Day. Anywhere they are placed indoors, they can brighten an entire room. Azaleas are also popular subjects for Bonsai culture.

There are hundreds of selections cultivated and the true azalea lover can, through choice of selection and proper cultural practices, have azaleas in bloom for most of the winter and spring. Here are a few of the most popular selections for container growing: Coral Bells (pink), Snow (white), Pink Pearl (pink), Sweetheart Supreme (reddish pink), Alaska (white), Pink Ruffles (pink), and Cherokee-White (white).

Locate azaleas where they will receive at least 4 hours of direct sunlight daily. When using artificial lighting, provide 800 foot-candles or more.

Soil for azaleas should be peaty loam. A good soil mix consists of 1 part sand or perlite, 1 part garden loam, and 2 parts leaf mold, peat moss, or finely shredded compost. Keep the soil evenly moist (not soaked) all the time. Provide medium humidity and a temperature range of 40° to 55° at night and 60° to 70° during the day.

Fertilize established plants monthly during the summer, but withhold fertilizer during the rest of the year. Use acid fertilizer which is available at garden supply stores. Do not fertilize new plants while they are in bloom. Yellowing leaves may indicate an iron deficiency. Add iron chelate or iron sulfate to the fertilizer solution, or, during fall, winter, and spring, apply either of these directly to the soil until the yellowing is corrected.

Propagate azaleas from stem cuttings of new growth taken during summer or early fall.

Repot azaleas after they finish blooming in the spring. When danger of frost is past, you may plant potted azaleas out in the garden. Tender selections will have to remain in containers and be brought back indoors before fall frost. Commercial azaleas that are forced into bloom for the Christmas holidays are subjected to temperatures of 45° to 50° for about 6 weeks before being forced.

Begonia, wax

Wax begonias are second only to African violets as the most popular flowering house plant in America. They are abundant producers, bearing small

Wax begonia *(B.* x *semperflorens-cultorum)*

waxy white, red, or pink single or double flowers. And their blooming season never seems to end. In much of the United States, they are transplanted in the garden during the summer, then dug up and potted for winter indoors. Many gardeners grow them from seed each year as an annual bedding plant.

Indoors, locate begonias in bright indirect light or in filtered sunlight during the growing season and in direct sun for 3 or 4 hours a day during winter. When using artificial lighting, provide at least 500 footcandles, a little more in winter.

Soil for begonias should be peaty loam. A good mix is 1 part sand or perlite, 1 part garden loam, and 2 parts leaf mold, peat moss, or finely ground compost. Allow soil to dry somewhat between thorough waterings. Keep plants on the dry side while they are dormant. Provide medium to high humidity and a temperature range of 50° to 60° at night and 65° to 70° during the day.

Fertilize established plants every other week during the growing season, but withhold fertilizer while the plants are dormant.

Propagate wax begonias from stem cuttings of new growth taken in summer or fall or from seeds sown any time.

Bougainvillea

Pleasing in every way, trailing bougainvilleas (*Bougainvillea* sp.) are especially lovely in hanging baskets or placed on an elevated shelf where they can cascade. Indoors or out, a display of hanging bougainvilleas can fill empty spaces on the deck or inside the home with spectacular bloom.

Depending on the selection, flowers may be red, pink, purple, orange, or white. Popular selections include:

'Scarlet O'Hara'	Red
'Texas Dawn'	Pink
'Camarillo Fiesta'	Pink or Gold
'Tahitian Gold'	Gold
'Barbara Karst'	Red

Locate bougainvilleas where they will receive at least 4 hours of direct sun each day. When using artificial lighting, provide 800 to 1000 footcandles. The plants are large so hanging containers must have strong support.

Soil for bougainvilleas should be loamy and well drained. Allow the soil to become partially dry between thorough waterings. Bougainvilleas prefer moderate humidity and a temperature range of 60° to 65° at night and 70° to 80° during the day.

Fertilize established plants every 2 to 4 weeks during the growing season (March to November), but withhold fertilizer during the winter dormant season. Do not feed newly potted or repotted plants for at least 1 month. Repot bougainvilleas in late winter or early spring.

Propagation is by stem cuttings taken during spring.

Christmas cactus

Christmas cactus (*Schlumbergera bridgesii*) is a multibranched plant with flat jointed stems 1¼ to 2

Bougainvillea

Christmas cactus *(Schlumbergera bridgesii)*

inches long and half that wide. It is an excellent house plant, especially suited for hanging baskets. In its native habitat it often lives on trees in a manner similar to that of some types of orchids. Being a jungle plant, it requires rich, porous soil with leaf mold and sand mixed in. Water Christmas cactus when the soil is dry and feed it at least once a month with mild liquid fertilizer during the growing season. For best results, withhold water and fertilizer after the plant finishes blooming. Do not allow the plant to dry out completely, but reduce watering considerably.

To induce blooming, take the plant outdoors in the fall, when night temperatures are between 50 and 55 degrees for several weeks. Do not water the plant while it is outdoors. When tiny flower buds appear at the tips of mature leaves, take the plant indoors and resume the regular watering schedule. If placed outdoors in early October, Christmas cactus should begin flowering sometime between Thanksgiving and Christmas.

Chrysanthemum

Chrysanthemums are one of the favorite potted flowering gift plants in America. Although less hardy than ordinary garden chrysanthemums, potted mums can be forced to bloom again the following winter holiday season. One caution, however: don't expect the mums you force at home to be as perfect as the florist's chrysanthemums, which are grown under the ideal conditions of a greenhouse. But with attention, patience, and proper care, your own home-forced chrysanthemums can be a source of satisfaction and pride.

After plants have flowered, cut stalks back to about 6 inches. Most pots of chrysanthemums contain several plants. Remove the rootball from the container, keeping it intact, and separate the plants. Pot them individually in 5- or 6-inch pots. Keep the plants in a cool, shaded place with a temperature around 60° and keep the soil moist. When new shoots appear, move the plants to a location where they will receive at least 4 hours of sun daily. Continue to keep them well watered.

In summer, sink the plants outside in a sunny place and feed them every 2 weeks with liquid fertilizer.

As with garden mums, pinching will be necessary to produce bushy plants. Pinch out the tip of each new shoot as it becomes 2 or 3 inches long. Remove only the soft portion of each shoot tip. Discontinue pinching around the middle of August.

Keep plants outside until frost threatens, then bring pots inside. Place them in a sunny window in the daytime and in a dark, cool place at night where they will receive no light, not even from a flashlight. The following process of chrysanthemums requires long nights of at least 12 to 14 hours of unin-

Chrysanthemums (*C. morifolium*)

terrupted darkness each night. After the buds begin to open, discontinue special nighttime treatment.

The success of this procedure can vary greatly and depends on the selection. On some selections, the flower buds may begin to open 8 to 10 weeks after pinching is discontinued. On others, it may take up to 14 weeks. In either case, patience and perseverance will be required.

Citrus

Citrus plants are delightful indoors because of their fragrance, their delicate white flowers, their dense evergreen leaves, and colorful fruit. The most popular indoor citrus plants are calamondin orange (x *Citrofortunella mitis*) and otaheite orange (*Citrus limonia*). They can be grown as 2- to 3-foot house plants. Lemons (*C. limon*) and grapefruit (*C. paradisi*) can also be grown indoors and are especially suited to home greenhouses and conservatories.

Locate citrus where it will receive a few hours of direct sun each day. A window on the south side is the best location. Under artificial lights, citrus must have 500 to 1200 footcandles for best results.

Soil for citrus should be loamy and well drained. Allow the soil to dry somewhat between thorough waterings. Provide high humidity by placing a pot of citrus on a tray filled with pebbles or 1-inch gravel and filling the tray with water until it almost touches the bottom of the pot. Daily misting of citrus plants is

also recommended. Temperatures should be 50° to 60° nights, 65° to 70° days.

Feed established plants in March, May, and August with a solution of fertilizer and water or general house plant food. Do not fertilize newly potted or repotted plants for at least 4 or 5 months. Repot overcrowded plants at any time of the year. Pinch back new growth to promote bushiness and to keep the plant compact.

Propagate citrus from stem cuttings or from seeds. Take cuttings during the fall and root them in moist sand or perlite. Seeds need no stratification and may be planted at any time. Do not allow them to dry out. When potting seedlings or rooted cuttings, place 3 or 4 plants together in a pot to enhance the bushiness of the mature plant. Seeds may also be sown in small clumps. Germination requires about 2 months.

Calamondin orange (x *Citrofortunella mitis*)

Fuchsia

The tropical fuchsia has become a popular house plant only in recent years. A humidity-loving plant from the jungle, fuchsia did not adapt to the dry, sometimes underlighted homes of our parents and grandparents. Modern hybridizers have developed plants that withstand increasingly drier environments.

Fuchsias bloom from late spring to mid-fall. The best displays are at the beginning of the bloom season and toward the end, as the weather once again cools off. Depending on the variety, flowers may be white, blue violet, purple, pink, or red. The most

Fuchsia

popular varieties used as house plants are trailing types which are utterly spectacular in hanging baskets.

Locate fuchsias in bright indirect sunlight during the summer and in direct sun for 4 hours a day the rest of the year. The selections Display and Cardinal will take more light than others. When using artificial lighting, provide at least 500 footcandles.

Water fuchsias every day. During hot, dry weather, fuchsias in hanging baskets may need to be watered twice a day. Mist the plants daily to satisfy their humidity needs. During the winter, the plants are dormant and require less moisture. Provide a temperature range of 50° to 60° at night and 65° to 75° during the day. Avoid drafty locations indoors and windy ones outdoors.

Fertilize plants every 2 to 4 weeks during the growing season. Do not fertilize new plants for at least 4 weeks. Repot crowded plants in late fall or early spring. After plants finish blooming in the fall, cut the stems back to 6 inches tall. New growth will begin to appear in January or February.

Insect enemies of fuchsias include aphids, whiteflies, and spider mites. Segregate infested plants immediately to curb the spread of the insects and apply necessary control measures (see Chapter Four, *Curing Plant Ailments*).

Propagate fuchsias from stem cuttings of new growth taken during the growing season.

Geranium

Among the oldest and most dependable flowering house plants is the common geranium (*Pelargonium* sp.). Its long bloom season (early spring through midfall) and large, velvety, sometimes scented leaves have made the geranium a favorite. In many parts of the country, potted plants are transplanted into the garden in the summer, then dug up and potted to come indoors in early fall.

Flowers may be single or double with many flowers to the cluster. Remove faded flowers frequently to encourage prolonged bloom. Pinching back the tips of new growth early in the season will stimulate dense branching and increased flower production.

Locate geraniums where they will receive at least 4 hours of direct sunlight daily. Under artificial lights, geraniums require at least 800 foot-candles.

Soil should be loamy and well drained. Let the soil dry somewhat between thorough waterings. Do not wet stems or leaves. Provide low to medium humidity and a temperature range of 50° to 60° at night and 65° to 75° during the day.

Fertilize established plants every 2 to 4 weeks from early spring to mid-fall, then every 4 to 6

Geranium (*Pelargonium* sp.)

weeks during the winter. Do not feed newly potted or repotted plants for at least 1 month. Geraniums bloom best when slightly potbound, so don't let their crowded appearance disturb you. The best time to repot severely crowded plants is early spring as new growth begins.

Because you may damage plants by allowing water to stand on stems or leaves, it is best to water plants by double potting or subirrigation.

Propagate geraniums at any time of year from stem cuttings or seeds.

Gloxinia

Anyone who has had success with African violets will want to try gloxinias *(Sinningia speciosa)*. These close relatives of African violets grow from tubers (swollen roots that store food and moisture) much like begonias and can bloom as spectacularly, given the proper care.

In addition to red, white, blue, purple, or pink flowers, some selections have pastel-colored flowers or speckled blossoms with contrasting borders. Some of the more popular selections include:

'Blanche de Meru'	Pink with white border
'Blue Chips'	Blue (double)
'Diana'	Pink with rose throat
'Emperor Frederick'	Scarlet with white border
'Etoile de Feu'	Scarlet
'Libelle'	White with red dots
'Mont Blanc'	White
'Monte Cristo'	Scarlet (double)
'Prince Albert'	Purple
'Queen Wilhelmina'	Pink
'Royal Flush'	Blue with white border (double)

Locate gloxinias in bright indirect light, but not in direct sunlight. Like African violets, gloxinias thrive under artificial lighting; provide at least 200 to 500 footcandles.

Soil should be peaty loam. Mix 1 part sand or perlite, 1 part loam, and 2 parts peat moss or leaf mold. Keep the soil slightly moist all the time. The temperature range for gloxinias should be 65° to 70° at night and 75° to 85° during the day. The higher the temperature, the greater the need for increasing humidity. In warm, dry homes, place pots of gloxinias on a pebble-filled tray that is filled with water nearly to the tops of the pebbles.

Fertilize established plants monthly during the growing season. Some species *(Sinningia pusilla* in particular) should receive less fertilizer and water during the winter. Do not fertilize newly potted or repotted plants for at least 1 month, 2 months if purchased during late fall and winter. Repotting should be done annually in early spring as new growth begins.

Propagate gloxinias at any time of the year from leaf cuttings or seeds. Plant tubers so that the top is even with or a little above the soil level. Water lightly until roots become established.

Jade plant

The popular jade plant *(Crassula argentea)* is a carefree, dependable plant with an interesting leaf and stem structure and a thick, aged-looking trunk. Given proper light, heat, and moisture, dense drooping clusters of white flowers are borne in spring. The flowers are sometimes a surprise to those who think of jade plant as a succulent foliage plant.

A native of South Africa, jade plant may grow to 4 or 5 feet tall in less than 10 years, and have a trunk diameter of 5 inches at soil level.

Locate jade plant where it will receive at least 4 hours of direct sunlight daily. Lacking such an ideal location, jade plant will also flourish in bright indirect sunlight. When using artificial lighting, provide 200 to 500 footcandles.

Soil for jade plant should be loamy and well drained. Allow the soil to become somewhat dry between thorough waterings. Provide medium humidity and a temperature range of 50° to 60° at

Gloxinia *(Sinningia speciosa)*

Jade plant (*Crassula argentea*)

night and 65° to 75° during the day for best results.

Fertilize established plants every 3 or 4 months, but wait at least a month before fertilizing newly potted or repotted plants. Repotting is required every 4 or 5 years, but seldom more frequently; jade plant thrives when it is pot-bound. When repotting does become necessary, it can be done at any time of year.

Propagate jade plant from leaf cuttings or stem cuttings taken at anytime of year. Allow stem cuttings to dry for 6 to 8 hours before placing them in the rooting medium.

Kalanchoe

Kalanchoe (*K. blossfeldiana*) is one of the most popular Christmas gift plants. Classed as succulents, the kalanchoes have opposite simple or compound leaves, often variegated, and bear clusters of scarlet flowers on drooping stalks. These members of the Stonecrop family are native to Malagasy. They are extremely frost tender and can be grown outside only in the southernmost areas of the United States.

During fall, winter, and spring, locate kalanchoe in a sunny window where it will receive at least 4 hours of direct sunlight daily. In the summer, it should receive bright light but not direct sun. Ideal temperature is 60 to 65 degrees at night and 70 to 75 degrees during the day. Kalanchoe needs moderate humidity and loamy, well drained soil. To avoid

crown rot, the major problem with this plant, water thoroughly when the soil is dry at a depth of 1 inch. Fertilize monthly with commercial house plant food at half the recommended rate.

As kalanchoes finish blooming, they become leggy and unkempt. Start new plants from stem cuttings rather than trying to keep old plants. After the cuttings have formed roots, pot them in a loamy mix.

To force blooms by Christmas, shelter kalanchoe from artificial light at night beginning in early September. Plants must have 14 or 15 hours of uninterrupted darkness each night for about 4 weeks. During the day, however, place them in their usual sunny location.

Here are some of the popular selections: Scarlet Gnome, Tetra Vulcan, Tom Thumb, and Brilliant Star, all with red flowers. The selection Jingle Bells has pendulous coral blossoms and is well suited for hanging baskets.

Poinsettia

Poinsettias (*Euphorbia pulcherrima*) are rather exacting in the cultural practices required to assure a second bloom, but with patience and attention, it can be done. After the poinsettia has finished blooming, begin to gradually withhold water. This

Kalanchoe (*K. blossfeldiana*), also called Panda plant.

Poinsettia (*Euphorbia pulcherrima*)

treatment causes the leaves to yellow and drop. Remove any other plants from the pot and store the dried-off poinsettia in a cool (50° to 60°), dry, dark place, such as a basement, until April or May. During this period, water the plant lightly to prevent the roots from drying out completely.

Bring the plant back into normal light conditions when weather has warmed, repot it, and cut the stem back to 6 inches; after all danger of frost has passed, sink the pot in the outdoor garden. Sink the pot where it will get plenty of sun and keep the plant well watered. Lift the pot from time to time to prevent growth of roots down into the soil outside the pot. As the plant becomes pot-bound, repot it in a larger pot, taking particular care not to damage the root system.

To keep poinsettias growing rapidly, feed them every 2 weeks with liquid fertilizer solution. Pinch out new shoots until early August, leaving only a few strong ones to develop. You may wish to root these cuttings in sand or perlite mixed equally with peat moss.

While potted plants are in the garden, be on the lookout for mealybugs which may cluster on the stem and at the base of leaves. If infestation is light, try to remove the insects by hand. If infestation continues or worsens, spray or dust plants with malathion, taking care not to let insecticide come in contact with flower bracts.

Bring plants back inside well in advance of fall frost. Provide a sunny location. Night temperature of about 60° and daytime temperature of 70° to 75° are ideal for producing good flowers.

Beginning early in October, shade plants completely for at least 14 to 16 hours a day. An undisturbed cellar should be dark and cool enough, but it is important that the plant receive no light—not even from a flashlight—during the night. You may need to cover the plant at night with some lightweight, tight cover as an added precaution. During the day, give it as much light as possible.

Avoid placing poinsettias in drafts and avoid rapid temperature fluctuations. Given correct cultural attention, poinsettias will hold their flowers for weeks.

Peace Plant

An excellent plant for the beginner, peace plant (*Spathiphyllum sp.*) thrives under difficult growing conditions, including partial neglect. The foliage is large and coarse; leaves are elliptic with smooth margins. Peace plant produces white flowers called spathes during the summer. The selection Mauna Loa blooms intermittently throughout the year.

Locate peace plant in bright light during the winter and in medium light the rest of the year. At no time should it receive direct sunlight. When using artificial lighting, provide at least 50 to 100 footcandles.

Soil should be peaty: 2 parts peat moss or leaf mold, 1 part loam, and 1 part sand or perlite. Keep the soil evenly moist. Medium to low humidity, as is found in most homes, is excellent for peace plant. Provide temperatures of 55 to 65 degrees at night and 70 to 80 degrees during the day.

Fertilize established plants every 2 months during

Peace plant (*Spathiphyllum sp.*)

the growing season. Overcrowded plants may be repotted at any time of year. To maintain the glossy appearance of the foliage, wipe the leaves at least monthly with a sponge.

Propagate peace plant at any time of year by dividing the roots.

Strawberry geranium, Strawberry begonia

Strawberry geraniums (*Saxifraga stolonifera*) are easy to grow and are popular terrarium and dish garden plants. They are also handsomely displayed in hanging baskets or strawberry jars.

Strawberry geraniums are small plants with rounded, velvety leaves that are attractively veined and have reddish undersides. Foliage is often variegated and resembles that of rex begonia, thus accounting for another common name of *Saxifraga stolonifera*, strawberry begonia. Small white flowers are borne irregularly in loose clusters on long stalks, but the main attraction is the foliage.

Locate strawberry geranium in medium to low light. When using artificial light, provide at least 400 to 500 footcandles.

Soil should be loamy. Allow soil to partially dry between thorough waterings. Strawberry geranium thrives in night temperatures of 50° to 65° and day

temperatures of 60° to 75°. Provide high humidity by placing pots of strawberry geraniums on a tray of pebbles filled with water.

Fertilize established plants monthly. Do not fertilize newly potted or repotted plants for at least 6 months. Repotting is best done in spring.

Propagate strawberry geraniums from runners. Snip off tiny young plants from the stolons (spreading stems with young plants at the end) and pot them individually. Strawberry geranium is a prolific mother; large plants produce as many as 3 dozen offsets in a single year.

Wax plant (*Hoya carnosa*)

Wax plant

Wax plant (*Hoya carnosa*) is valued for its thick, dark green leaves and long-lasting, fragrant flowers. This native of southern China is a trailing or twining vine that bears small, star-shaped flowers in axillary clusters in early summer.

Locate wax plant in medium to full light for best flower production. Wax plants tolerate low-light conditions but will produce few, if any, flowers. When using artificial light, provide at least 200 to 500 footcandles.

Soil for wax plant should be loamy. Keep the soil moist during summer and fall, but reduce watering by half during later winter and spring to enhance the flowering process. Provide night temperatures of 60 to 65 degrees and day temperatures of 70 to 80 degrees.

Fertilize established plants every two to three weeks from late spring to early fall, but withhold fertilizer during the rest of the year. Repot crowded plants at any time of the year.

Do not remove the leafless spurs that appear from the main stems; these are the stalks on which new flowers will be borne.

Wax plants are easy to train on a pole or moss stick; or place them in an elevated position where they can cascade.

Propagate at any time of the year from stem cuttings or by air-layering.

Strawberry geranium (*Saxifraga stolonifera*), also called Strawberry begonia.

FLOWERING HOUSE PLANTS

Latin name	Common names	Watering	Light	Temp.	Humidity	Repotting soil
Acalypha hispida	Chenille plant	moist all the time	FS; DS best	60°–75°	medium	loamy
Aeschynanthus radicans	Lipstick plant	moist all the time	FS 4 hrs.; DS in winter	65°–75°	medium	peaty loam
Ananas comosus Variegatus	Pineapple	moist all the time	4 hrs. DS/day	60°–70°	medium	peaty loam
Aphelandra squarrosa	Zebra plant	moist spring to fall; dry between waterings in winter	FS;no DS	60°–75°	high	peaty loam
Azalea sp.	Azalea, see page 81					
Begonia x semperflorens-cultorum	Wax begonia, see page 81					
Begonia coccinea	Angel-wing begonia					
Beloperone guttata	Shrimp plant	dry between thorough waterings	4 hrs. DS/day	50°–75°	medium	loamy
Bougainvillea sp.	Bougainvillea, see page 82					
Capsicum annuum	Ornamental pepper	moist all the time	best in DS	60°–70°	medium	loamy
Chrysanthemum sp.	Chrysanthemum, see page 83					
x Citrofortunella mitis	Calamondin orange, see page 84					
Citrus sp.	Orange, see page 84 Grapefruit Lemon					
Crassula argentea	Jade plant, see page 86					
Cyclamen sp.	Florist's cyclamen	moist all the time	FS	40°–65°	medium	peaty loam
Euphorbia pulcherrima	Poinsettia, see page 87					
Fortunella margarita	Nagami kumquat	dry between thorough waterings	4 hrs. DS/day	50°–75°	medium	loamy
Fuchsia sp.	Fuchsia, see page 84					
Gardenia jasminoides	Gardenia Cape jasmine	moist all the time	4 hrs. DS/day	60°–72°	high	peaty loam
Hoya carnosa	Wax plant, see page 89					
Hydrangea macrophylla	French hydrangea Bigleaf hydrangea	very moist	FS	55°–75°	medium	peaty loam
Impatiens sp.	Impatiens Sultana	moist all the time	DS to low	60°–70°	medium	peaty loam
Kalanchoe blossfeldiana	Kalanchoe, see page 87 Panda plant					

Latin name	Common names	Watering	Light	Temp.	Humidity	Repotting soil
Lantana camara	Common lantana	dry partly between thorough waterings	4 hrs. DS/day	55°–70°	medium	loamy
Lilium longiflorum	Easter lily	dry partly between thorough waterings; moist while blooming	FS	40°–70°	medium to high	loamy
Osmanthus fragrans	Sweet olive	moist all the time	FS or medium	50°–70°	medium	loamy
Oxalis sp.	Oxalis	moist all the time	4 hrs. DS/day	50°–70°	medium	loamy
Pelargonium sp.	Geranium, see page 85					
Primula malacoides	Fairy primrose	slightly moist all the time	FS	40°–70°	medium	loamy
Saintpaulia sp.	African violet, see page 80					
Saxifraga stolonifera	Strawberry geranium, see page 89 / Strawberry begonia					
Schlumbergera bridgesii	Christmas cactus, see page 82					
Sinningia speciosa	Gloxinia, see page 86					
Solanum pseudocapsicum	Jerusalem cherry	dry partly between thorough waterings	DS to medium	50°–70°	medium	loamy
Spathiphyllum sp.	Peace plant / Spathiphyllum	moist all the time	low; FS in winter	60°–70°	medium	peaty loam
Sprekelia formosissima	Aztec lily	moist during growing season; dry in winter	4 hrs. DS/day	60°–70°; 40°–65°	medium	loamy
Strelitzia reginae	Bird-of-paradise / Strelitzia	slightly dry between thorough waterings	4 hrs. DS/day	50°–70°	medium	loamy
Thunbergia alata	Black-eyed Susan vine	moist all the time	4 hrs. DS/day	50°–70°	medium	loamy

Watering: Moist in this context means do not soak. A plant that should be moist at all times should never be wet and never be dry.

Cactus and other succulents use very little water in winter. Use only enough to keep them from shriveling; about 2 to 3 weeks between waterings.

Light: DS means direct sunlight, usually at least 4 hours daily. FS means filtered sunlight or a bright room. Medium can often be found in north or east facing windows. Low light means the plant will tolerate very little light, but in most cases would prefer more.

Temperature: the lowest temperature listed is the coolest night-time temperature recommended and the higher one is the high-est recommended daytime temperature. Somewhere be-tween the two should suit your home.

Humidity: Low and medium mean the conditions found in most homes. High means place the plants on a tray of pebbles filled nearly to the top of the pebbles with water. Misting the plants daily is also recommended.

Repotting soil: Loamy means equal parts garden loam, peat moss, and sand or perlite. Leaf mold and finely ground compost are good substitutes for peat moss. Sandy loam means 2 parts sand or perlite to 1 part loam and 1 part peat moss. Peaty soil is rich in organic matter, composed of 1 part sand, 1 part loam, and 2 parts peat.

Leaf Shapes and Arrangements

Botanists, in an effort to describe leaf shapes, leaf margins, and arrangements of leaves on stems, have invented terms that often baffle the amateur.

To clarify these terms as they are used in our text, we include here a graphic explanation of some frequently encountered descriptive terms.

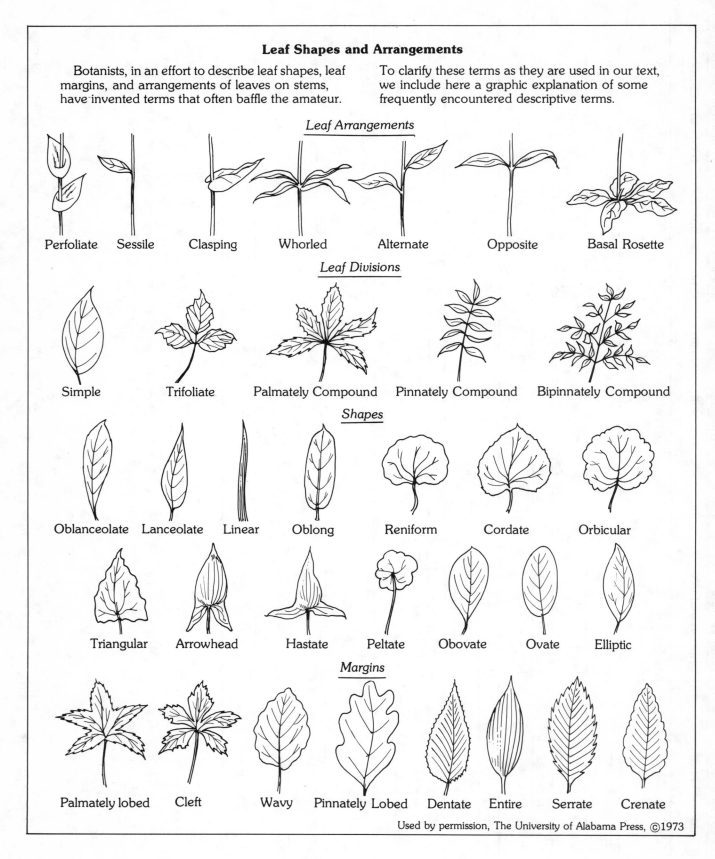

Leaf Arrangements

Perfoliate Sessile Clasping Whorled Alternate Opposite Basal Rosette

Leaf Divisions

Simple Trifoliate Palmately Compound Pinnately Compound Bipinnately Compound

Shapes

Oblanceolate Lanceolate Linear Oblong Reniform Cordate Orbicular

Triangular Arrowhead Hastate Peltate Obovate Ovate Elliptic

Margins

Palmately lobed Cleft Wavy Pinnately Lobed Dentate Entire Serrate Crenate

Glossary

Air-layering. A method of propagating (reproducing) plants by which roots are formed on a partial cut in the main stem of the plant. The rooted portion is then detached and potted separately.

Blight, blighting. A general term for fungus diseases which usually cause spotting and wilting of foliage.

Bottle garden. A terrarium that uses a bottle as a container.

Bulb, bulbous plant. An enlarged portion of root or subsurface stem in which plant nutrient is stored. The term bulb may also refer to a plant that has this type of root or stem.

Crown. Top portion of root system where roots meet stem.

Cutting. A section of leaf, stem, or root used to start new plants. The cutting is placed in sand, peat moss, or other rooting media where it forms new roots.

Division, dividing. The process of dividing the root system of a plant to form two or more new plants.

Dormant, dormancy. Being at rest or in a period of non-growth. Many plants enter a dormant period during winter.

Double potting. Placing a potted plant in a larger pot with sphagnum moss or other moisture-retentive material between the walls of the two containers.

Epiphyte, epiphytic. An "air-borne" plant whose roots assimilate moisture and nutrients from the air and need no soil medium. Many bromeliads are epiphytes.

Fertilizer, liquid. A solution of water and soluble (dissolvable) fertilizer.

Fertilizer, slow-release. Any fertilizer that releases nutrients slowly to the plant.

Foot-candle. A measure of light; the amount of light cast by a candle on a surface 1 foot away.

Forcing bloom. Usually referring to bulbs and shrubs, the process of stimulating bloom out of season.

Fungicide. An agent, usually chemical, used to kill fungi.

Germination. The earliest stage of formation of a plant from seed, i.e., when the seed "sprouts."

Hardening. Gradual acclimatization of a plant to any change of environment.

Insecticide. An agent, usually chemical, used for killing insects.

Leaf mold. Partially decayed leaves.

Leggy. Characterized by long, spindly stems.

Loamy soil. A potting soil of equal parts loam, peat moss, and sand (or perlite).

Misting, foliar feeding. Spraying leaves of a plant with water.

Mulch. Any material placed around the base of a plant to discourage weeds and conserve moisture. Common mulch materials include sawdust, pine straw, shredded bark, and compost among others.

Nematocide. An agent, usually chemical, for killing nematodes. Nematodes are microscopic soil organisms, many species of which are destructive to plants.

Offsets. Small plants that are produced at the base of a mature plant.

Organic matter. A general term for plant material at various stages of decomposition.

Peat moss. Partially decomposed sphagnum moss, used as a soil additive and valued particularly for its moisture-holding capacity: it can retain 6 to 10 times its weight in water.

Peaty soil. A soil mix containing 1 part loam, 1 part sand (or perlite), and 2 parts peat moss, leaf mold, or other decomposed organic matter.

Perlite. A white granular material derived from silica; used as a substitute for sand in potting and rooting media.

Pinching. Process of pinching off portions of stems to remove spindly growth and stimulate branching.

Planter. A large container, often stationary, for growing plants.

Plunging (pots). Burying pots in soil up to their rims; a recommended practice for plants that will be left unattended for a week or more.

Pot-bound. Severe constriction of plant roots in a container. Pot-bound plants should be repotted.

Propagate, propagation. To stimulate plant reproduction. Common methods include seeds, cuttings, runners, offsets, and air-layering.

Pruning. The judicious removal of parts of a plant to encourage new growth, eliminate dead or diseased parts, or train to a desired form.

Raceme. An elongated main stem that bears flowers.

Repotting. Transferring a plant to a larger container when the plant becomes pot-bound or if destructive soil insects are detected.

Rooting. Stimulating root formation on a cutting taken from a plant.

Rooting medium. Any material in which roots may form on cuttings taken from a plant. Common rooting media include sand, perlite, peat moss, and sphagnum moss.

Runner. A plantlet borne by a mature plant on an elongated stem.

Sandy soil. A soil mix consisting of 1 part loam, 1 part peat moss or leaf mold, and 2 parts sand or perlite.

Sphagnum moss. Dried mosses found in bogs.

Stolon. A vinelike stem that grows along the ground or just under the surface and produces a new plant at its tip.

Subirrigating. Watering from the bottom of a container, usually done by placing a pot in a saucer or pan filled with water. Moisture is drawn up through the drainage hole in the bottom of the pot.

Succulent. A plant with thick, fleshy leaves and stems in which moisture is stored.

Sucker. A shoot that arises at the base of a mature plant.

Terrarium. An enclosed glass or plastic case in which plants are grown.

Top-dressing. Removing the topmost soil from a large container and replacing it with fresh soil. This is a common practice with plants that are too large to repot. Excess root growth is also trimmed.

Variegated foliage. Foliage characterized by an edging of white or yellow on leaf margins.

Vermiculite. A light, micalike material sometimes used as a rooting medium.

Index